APRICOT BLOOMS

in the

DESERT

by Edward Payne

puBLished By

fanfare
Books

stratford, ontario

The Apricot Blooms In The Desert
Copyright © 2004, 2008 by Edward Payne

Second edition (2008) edited by John Lederman
First edition (2004) edited by Meg Macintyre and Stephen Newman (Wingate Press)

Design and Layout by John Lederman
Back cover design by Everett Newman

Typeface
Titles: Didot
Text: Garamond

Printed in Canada
(2nd printing)
by the Aylmer Express Ltd.

Library and Archives Canada Cataloguing in Publication

Payne, Edward, 1926-
The Apricot Blooms In The Desert / Edward Payne.

ISBN 0-9735977-4-7

1. Payne, Edward, 1926- . I. Title.

PS8631.A954A67 2004   C818'.603   C2004-905796-0

Preface

When I first began writing this book, it was meant as a journal for my daughter Vicky. I have always regretted that my father, Cecil Payne, who had such a varied and adventurous life, had not written some sort of record or diary. I would love to have read his recounting of life as a schoolboy, pre-nineteen fourteen, or life in the nightmare of the trenches. He told me stories and shared anecdotes about those times, but I longed for more. Suffice it to say that I have made friends laugh to this day repeating tales.

The other inspirational spark was planted years ago, when my first wife, Vianne, said in reply to my complaint that I had read everything in the library, "Teddy, why don't you write your own book?"

This book is presented in segments, in a disconnected fashion because it highlights the very pivotal earlier experiences in my life that are not necessarily consecutive. This is how I remember these times in my life and in memory; absolute facts are often obscured or coloured with emotion. My life up to the early sixties is described only as those moments that had some influence, good or bad, upon my actions and personality.

I have had such luck. One thing always led to another, as is common to most. However, I suspect I had more jam in the doughnut than I deserved. I was fortunate in discovering early in life that it is wise to respect one's elders, to be aware of their superior knowledge, and to benefit by listening. My path was eased for me along the way by influential men and women who wanted to help me. For that, I am truly grateful.

As to the publishing of this book, the story bears telling again...

The fact that this book and its sequel *The Streets of Odeon,* were put together and published at all is again entirely due to being in the right place at the right time...

I sit in the park here in Stratford every summer and display and sell small watercolours to tourists. One day two terribly nice people came through and were friendly and kind. They had just moved to town. In the conversation I asked them what they did.

"We are book publishers," they say.

I say, "I've written a book."

They say, "Love to read it."

Politeness, I think, but I gave them the whole mess, a rambling incoherent account of my luck in life, roughly from the thirties, when little, on. They read it and loved it.

They worked and worked and produced *The Apricot Blooms in the Desert.* I was so proud. Stacey and Stephen Newman, my first publishers, changed my life and I shall always love them and be grateful.

The Apricot Blooms in the Desert unexpectedly did well enough that the first run entirely sold out. For this second edition it was decided to re-work it slightly with some different editing and layout and pictures.

Again, thank you to all the marvellous people who encouraged and helped me and told me when I was doubtful, that I could write, laughed at my silly stories and my absurdities: to Bob Newland, my present publisher in this risky and sometimes frightening, but exhilarating adventure; to John Lederman, my present editor and friend; to Kelley Teahen for her wise advice about tone, voice, and narrative, and her copy-editing; to Christopher Plummer for his kind and generous words of encouragement; and to the many others in my life who have helped and with whom I had the precious experiences to write about and to share with others.

The

APRICOT BLOOMS

in the

DESERT

A Literary Memoir
Part One

"Every garden should have a path that leads nowhere..."

Percy Marriott Payen-Payne

It was nineteen sixty. The DC3 droned across the flat mid-western fields. Gazing out of the window, watching the shadows of clouds follow each other, I thought again of the contrasts between America and England. We had been flying now for the same period of time it would take to go from London to Edinburgh, and yet the countryside had not changed perceptibly. It all looked the same, no hills or dales, no undulating moor, no hedge, no copse, paddock, or water meadow.

This was Indiana, where gardens are called "backyards" and wire fences criss-cross a kind of no man's land, with the outposts signaling to each other in tawdry daylight neon. The heartland, the all-American Town.

Did I imagine it, or was that bolt unscrewing itself out of the engine cover on my side of the engine? Certainly something nasty seemed to be happening. I had never felt comfortable in DC3s since seeing *Lost Horizon*. I always expected an Oriental-faced pilot to turn at the critical moment and grin malevolently at me. As I felt around for seatbelt and whiskey flask, the stewardess approached. She was round-faced, round-bodied, pink and bland – very comforting when one felt imminent disaster approaching.

"Can I help you?" she asked.

I pointed out of the window at the errant screw which seemed to be revolving faster then before.

"I think the engine's falling off."

"Oh, what an imagination. Nothing to worry about." The teeth gleamed. The full shiny lips smiled. The eyes were bored and blank.

"This plane has been flying since World War II and not a screw has come out yet. You'll have to put that liquor away. It's against the FAA rules. And please fasten your seatbelt. We're about to land at Fort Wayne."

This casual, confident attitude again seemed to underline the difference between us. It was so, so American. I used to dream of the golden land, blue waters, stucco and palm, tanned approachable girls, boulevarded terraces, bountiful refrigerators and classy bars. Oh, Odeon Cinema what you have to answer for: those wet, dank evenings on Haverstock Hill in November struggling with mackintosh and newspapered fish and chips. You hadn't prepared me for the blowing grey papers and cardboard coffee cups of a January day in Indiana...

hooting, the fog-wrapped woods
glisten in blackened misery,

snow patched and threadbare
with naked twig a nursery

for all that is beyond the eye
alerted for that ancient cry...

"You'll have to control those bloody horses," an Inspector of the Metropolitan Police yelled at the two mounted Bobbies whose horses were rearing and whinnying with fright. Three Hawker Hurricanes had just roared low over the crowd at Hendon. The dappled green and brown low-wing planes were the first to fly and had come from nowhere. The only sign of their approach had been the skittish behaviour of the normally unflappable horses. The crowd "oohed" and "aahed," waved, clapped, and cheered.

It was the nineteen thirty-eight Hendon Air Show, the last before the war, and the crowd seemed to sense it. Trenches were being dug in the parks. A film played of the H.G. Well's story *A Shape of Things to Come* in which too-realistic scenes depicted safe, sane, middle-class families being blown up, together with landmarks like Piccadilly Circus. It was all very upsetting. My father was gnashing at the bit to get back into the army. A war would be his only chance of becoming an officer and gentleman again.

"If we don't take a crack at them now, we'll miss the bus," my father would say.

I gripped his hand as he walked me down the ordered ranks of planes, describing each one's special characteristics. We looked over Hawker Furies, biplanes with two-seater open cockpits, Hinds and Harts, Gamecocks and Gladiators. All fine for keeping enemy heads down on the northwest frontier, but after seeing the Hurricanes and knowing what was on the other side of the North Sea thanks to reports by the two-penny boys' papers of the time, Triumph and Champion, Skipper and Hotspur, hardly suitable for total modern war.

Going home that night, packed in the underground train that smelled of damp clothes, beer, and sweat, I thought about the following day. Monday. Back to school. I'd had a row with my best friend and I was trying to think of a way of making amends. I looked up at my father's hulking and stern implacability in his stained Burberry coat. He was every inch a gent fallen on bad times with his unclipped moustache, tobacco yellowed and prematurely white, and his slightly glaucous, watery blue eyes. He'd had a few with a couple of army chums he'd bumped into at the airfield and there was no way I could talk to him about my affairs. Besides being totally unapproachable in this gently inebriated state, his mind might be anywhere of a thousand places from Singapore to the Egyptian desert. Certainly it was not on the Tube train under Highgate.

"Here's where we get off Daddy," I said as we pulled into Belsize Park.

"Daddy," I repeated, "Home."

"What, what?" he snapped. "What the bloody hell?"

"It's our station."

"Oh Christ-all-bloody-mighty!"

His coat became caught in the closing door as I pulled out onto the platform.

"Sodding bloody buggery!!! That's my best coat. You should have warned me earlier. I was resting my eyes."

We got on the lift with the rest of the passengers who were all looking at Dad with some apprehension. He had what we used to call his "Colonel Blimp" look on his face. Usually florid, his complexion now was positively beetroot. What with his height, military bearing, staring eye, and clearly audible comments about the London Passenger Transport Board and what they could do with their fucking doors that closed too quickly, he was a formidable sight. I pitied any German soldier who ever met my Dad coming out of a pub.

It was about six o'clock when we got home. We lived, in those days, in the basement flat of a large Victorian house in Hampstead. It was ugly but comfortable, all the furniture second hand, and that bought on the never-never. The smell of toast and tea came from the kitchen and my sister came out carrying plates of crumpets and Scotch pancakes. Being a Sunday, we were having a special tea.

In London before the war, one could still buy from the "muffin man" who used to walk around the streets with a tray balanced on his head. He would ring a bell to attract attention and we children would be sent out to buy. Those were great evenings, fog and cold outside, fire crackling, warmth, tea, family, and the children's hour on the wireless inside.

With a large teapot, cosy-covered in one hand and a plate of fruit cake in the other, my mother plonked down in front of the fire. She asked about our trip to Hendon. Between mouthfuls of crumpet I described the pageant, "...and Daddy met some of his old pals, and... " This part was interrupted by my father who didn't want Mum to know about this aspect of the day. She did not approve of his drinking, especially as cash was hard to come by.

He asked me if I had any homework to do. I replied that I had, but that it could wait. My father, sensing more treachery on my part, pressed his advantage, insisting that I depart to do it immediately. I opened my mouth to protest, but catching his eye, thought better of it. So grabbing a handful of toast and cake and surreptitiously kicking my sister who was giggling in the corner, I walked out of the room.

Madeleine was my sister, and being a girl, was an odd sort of person given to dramatic poses, dreamy looks, and a complete indifference to my Hornby train set. She and her best friend were currently and collectively in love with the local cinema's organ player. They used to moon around the back of the Odeon in the hope of seeing him. In between these flights of fancy they would write copious letters to star magazines for signed photographs of their favourite of the day. Needless to say, these activities filled me with disgust and only confirmed my opinion that all girls were like flies; there seemed to be no reason at all why God had put them on the Earth.

The homework was awful, totally incomprehensible, and to my mind a complete waste of time. What good would decimals and vulgar fractions be when facing the screaming, savage horde on the blood-soaked desert, or the crook in the Los Angeles apartment with the rather large gun? I had not made up my mind at this stage in life whether I was going to be an African explorer or a private detective in America. In either case, I had other fish to fry than to swot away at mathematics.

It was September, cold, grey, and cheerless. I wound my reluctant way down Belsize Road towards school. I was a day boy at a Preparatory School near home, and would walk the few miles by a different and circuitous route every day, principally because, in our school uniform, being a pink cap and a pink blazer, we were the target of every lay-about and loafer in the neighbourhood, who upon setting beady eyes on us would yell, "Hey Nancy, wait for me!" Then if they caught us, would box our ears and generally make life unpleasant.

It was a very nasty experience, however, it stood many of us in good stead later when we went to war, especially those who became soldiers. It was like street and house-to-house fighting. We would creep up to a corner and peer discreetly 'round, and then, if all clear, we would scuttle up to the next street, and so on. Getting home was quite an adventure, and once there (over tea) we would plan the next day's course through the territory. If we knew that it would be impossible to avoid gangs, we would wear a raincoat and stuff our caps into our pockets.

This particular day the louts were absent, so I arrived without incident. I bumped into my friend Hadwen almost immediately. He was obviously pleased to see me, and chortled about his walk in that morning. Hadwen came from a different direction than me, and had his own particular hellfire corner to cope with every day. Apparently he had outwitted his nemesis. He had disguised himself by wearing his jacket inside out, disarraying his hair, and putting on what we used to call his idiot expression. Unfortunately, just as he was demonstrating this for our benefit, Mr. Glazer, our housemaster, came around the corner to be faced with this grimace at its apogee.

"When you have finished making an ass of yourself, you will immediately go to your classroom and start writing a hundred times I will not make disgusting faces at my housemaster again," he said icily, not pausing in his stride, with his gown flowing behind as he swept on down the corridor.

Mr. Glazer, it was rumoured, had taken part in an expedition to Everest and was something of an outdoor man still. He would, when in a receptive mood, describe how he had led the way up the western rim, and occasionally got carried away to the extent that he would actually climb the classroom wall and hang from the moulding with one hand, resembling a demented ape.

One marvellous day, Mr. Wadden, the headmaster, walked in while Glazer was in full cry (he had just pulled out his imaginary ice pick and was calling for his lead Sherpa played by Hilton Minimus). Wadden, who was something of an eccentric himself (he often wore two coats, two sweaters, and now and again two ties) peered up at the mountaineer.

"Ah Glazer, I see you have not forgotten your earlier skills. However, I suggest your more advanced years and position of some dignity here call for more decorum on your part." With that he walked out just as Glazer lost his grip and fell to the floor. We all collapsed in laughter.

We were studying Latin, a subject I was fairly good at initially. Then, for some reason, when doing exams later in the year, I managed to fail Latin with the lowest marks in the school's history, thus gaining something of a reputation as an unusually dull boy. This stigma was to follow me for the rest of my school years, in spite of my progress in other areas of study such as history, geography, English, and art.

Mr. Wadden would, on the rare occasion that he noticed any of the boys at all, contemplate me with a disconsolate expression and say, "Oh Payne, a great disappointment. Italian mother you know, and yet a complete dunce at Latin."

The months, and finally the year, passed. Christmas nineteen thirty-eight came and went. The Christmas holidays were not unusual. We got our expected family gift from our grandparents, a crate of Jaffa oranges. This was a traditional gift to the family for reasons I was never able to fathom, as none of us particularly liked oranges. Perhaps there was some obscure Biblical connection, something to do with the Holy Land, especially as we had in the early thirties spent some time in Palestine, where father worked for an American oil company. Whatever the reason, here were the inevitable fruits. I also was given additions to my train set, and Madeleine, who was three years my senior, got new clothes.

Nineteen thirty-nine began ominously. Little did we know how much worse it was going to get before it was over. Early in February the weather, which had been relatively mild, turned nasty. Storm days followed one after another. The damp and cold finally got through all the flannel I had to wear and brought me down. I spent the next few days in a never-never-land of fever and delirium, and apparently only just made it. The first thing I remember was the doctor telling my mother that I would be able to have lots of blanc-mange, jellies, and custards. This cheered me up considerably, and after a few bed baths (lukewarm wet face cloths), long days in bed, and the diet prescribed, I made a complete recovery. The illness put me back badly at school. I had to really study to catch up.

At the end of the summer holidays, endless warm and sunny days chasing around Hampstead Heath, climbing trees, and puffing on a Player's Weights cigarettes when no one was looking, my father came home one evening with a worried look on his face. He and our mother talked in low voices in the bedroom, and when they came out, Mother said she and Daddy thought we should go and stay with our Grandfather for a while. We didn't ask for any other explanation as we both enjoyed going to stay in the country, and there was something about the whole atmosphere of the moment that made further enquiries seem unwelcome.

The packing was feverish and nervous. Mother was in a very excitable state of mind and Father was irritable and impatient. I couldn't understand why I couldn't take all my train set with me, and Madeleine was bleating about her boyfriend.

The taxi came and we bundled off to King's Cross. We had been this way many times on calmer occasions, but this time it was all different.

The station was packed, as were all the streets, and the trip through east London was hectic and tense. My father went off in search of tickets and we went to look for food. We bought ham sandwiches, a couple of small pork pies, some potato crisps, and lemonade. Daddy had been gone an age and Mummy was becoming frantic. We had no idea of times of trains and began to wonder if we would miss whatever one we were supposed to catch. Though I was hungry, I somehow couldn't eat. People rushed backwards and forwards, porters shoved and swore, and pets in hampers whimpered and snarled.

Finally, Daddy turned up waving tickets and shouting, "Hurry, we don't have a moment to lose! The train leaves in a couple of minutes."

We rushed after him. It wasn't easy with the crowds, but with his height and bearing he was able to push his way through and we followed. The platform we were leaving from was jammed with service men. There seemed to be troops from every regiment and corps in the army, as well as sailors an airmen. Confusion reigned.

We were finally deposited in a third-class compartment, which we shared with an elderly couple in tweeds, three artillery men, one of whom picked his nose in the most revolting manner, a bearded sailor fast asleep in spite of all the noise and pandemonium, and lastly, a young girl of about sixteen who had been crying and who was now gazing fixedly at her ticket.

Mum was now crying and even Dad was snuffling, pulling at his moustache, and saying, "What, what, what," which he always did when nervous or upset.

The engine gave a warning hoot and doors all along the train began to slam. The guard's whistle blew and Mum gave a last hug to Madeleine. Daddy, pursing his lips, blew us both a kiss. The door shut. I leaned out of the window and gripped his hand.

"Be good, and look after Madeleine," he said gruffly.

The train jerked and started to move. He let go my hand and stood still. I watched him until the crowd moving around hide him from view. I shut the window and sat back.

"I wonder what it's all about."

"I think *that*," Madeleine pointed at the newspaper the tweedy gent was reading. "POLAND INVADED. GERMAN TROOPS IN ACTION AGAINST POLISH FRONTIER FORCES" read the headlines of the sheet facing us. I looked out of the coal-grimed window.

The train had left the suburbs behind and was gathering speed. We rattled across points and passed through a station. I noticed workmen dismantling the station sign for Hitchin... .

It was the sudden jerk of the train that woke me up. I looked at my watch. It had stopped. I glanced over to the others. Everyone was still asleep.

I noticed the older couple had disappeared. They must have got off. It was quite dark now and I wondered where we were. The line went through a market town called Beccles, where we were to be met. I shook Madeleine.

We started getting our things together. We seemed to be approaching a town, a few indistinct lights glimmered through the darkness. Then we were obviously entering a built-up area. Although blackout regulations had come in effect on an unofficial basis, not many people bothered about them, so the place was well lit up. We clumsily managed our things and proceeded off the train.

"Well, you two must be exhausted." This was Constance, our step-grandmother. We had met her once before when only an indistinct impression had been made. We had heard lots about her from the grown-ups, according to whom she was a horror incarnate. She did look formidable and I shook in my shoes. She was tall, and standing there in the weak light of a station yard lamp, vaguely sinister. She wore a heavy full-length fur coat and fur hat which seemed to accentuate even more the impression of great height. The fur glistened in the reflected glow to form an aura around her. Her face was small and well-shaped with a very red, firm mouth. The eyes were the arresting feature. They were the eyes of a cat, no, less domestic than a cat, more perhaps like a lynx, a pale bright green colour, sharp and watchful.

After perfunctory pecks on the cheek, she said, "Come on, the car's over here." We followed apprehensively to where a large, dark-coloured car was parked.

"Teddy, you get in front with me. Madeleine, you'll sit in the back. You'll find a rug to put over your knees."

Constance switched the ignition on and the car purred luxurious life as we glided out of the station gates.

"Well, tell me all the news from London. We wonder what's happening."

Constance at this time, was probably in her mid-forties. She had married our grandfather almost immediately after the death of his first wife, our paternal grandmother, who, because of her southern Irish extraction, had had a profound influence on the religious penchants of her family. This was a trend that had been strengthened by the marriage of our father to an Italian. Madeleine and I were by now pillars of the Anglo-Catholic community. In this papist atmosphere Constance was a nonconformist: low church, bitterly anti-clerical, ambitious, and ruthless. Anyone born outside Birmingham, her home, was foreign. Anyone born abroad was a "Wog." It was rumoured that she had been a mannequin (a model), a profession viewed then with about as much esteem as a prostitute. Despite everything, Constance had always been reasonably cordial to Mother and Father, and not especially unkind to us.

"Daddy thinks war is coming soon, and we are stay with you until other arrangements can be made."

"Yes, I know. Cecil called earlier and told us. It's really very inconvenient. I don't know how the servants will manage, I'm sure. One has such a difficult time keeping maids, especially since all *this* bother started. They are all running off and joining the land army or the WAAFS or some such nonsense. It's all really too bad."

"Well, we'll try not to be a nuisance, won't we Madeleine?" I was answered by a loud snore from the back seat.

We had been driving for about half an hour. Constance drove efficiently, with little movement and no fuss. This was a woman very much in control. We came to a stop sign, paused, and turned to the left, moving up a narrow, hedge-lined, tree-lined road. It wound around in an aimless fashion for a few miles. I caught glimpses of some tumbled fields lit by a fitful moon. On the whole, the countryside seemed quite flat and low-lying.

Constance braked slightly and changed gears. We slowed and turned sharply to the right, passing through an open gateway. The tyres crunched on gravel. We were now on a long curving driveway. On either side, tall clipped hedges of yew loomed over the car. The headlights illuminated an expanse of open lawn with decorative urns dotted at intervals along a low stone wall. The car swung to the left and the house came into sight. The headlights and weak moonlight showed it to be a substantial brick two-storey Georgian mansion, graceful and elegant. The front door was open, and light from within flooded out.

An erect figure with a walking stick was outlined there. It was Percy Marriott Payen-Payne, Major Ret'd.

Sherwood Foresters, and unofficial squire of the village of Haddiscoe, Norfolk. He was about seventy then, but in excellent health and spirits. A surveyor in his younger days, he had spent several years in that profession with the London Midland & Scottish Railway. He was quite an innovative man and had several up-to-date ideas about agricultural matters. In fact, he owned a model market garden there, not large, but productive. He was a keen sportsman, an excellent shot, and had won a quantity of silverware to attest to that fact. His stamp collection was well known and he probably possessed the finest collection of grandfather clocks in the country.

"Well, well Teddy, how you've grown!" I was the first out of the car and he came towards me and gave me a hug. Madeleine emerged from the back of the car.

"Grandad, it's lovely to see you, and so super to be here."

"My dears, come in. I'm sure you must be tired. Mrs. Beaver has prepared something for you to eat."

We followed him into the house. Constance had driven the car around the back where the stables, now used as garages, were. We sat down to biscuits and hot Ovaltine while Grandad regarded us with a look of affectionate bewilderment. It was now very late, and after the plates and cups were cleared away by a ruddy-cheeked girl in service who winked at me, we were taken up to our rooms.

The guest bedrooms were in the back, in a part of the house dating from the time of Queen Anne. It was reputed to be haunted.

After the initial restlessness that one has in strange

rooms and beds, I slept soundly and probably would have continued sleeping if my curtains had not been drawn with a flourish, bathing the room in bright sunlight. A different maid to the one last night put a cup of tea and a digestive biscuit by my bed.

She was dressed in a light blue uniform with white apron and cap. She was quite pretty, with bright blue eyes and rosy cheeks. Everyone here looked so healthy.

"Good mornin' Mast' Teddy. It's breakfast in 'arf an 'aah."

"Good morning ...er, ...er, Miss, ...er... . What is your name?"

"Christine, youn' Mast'."

"Thanks Christine, I'll be down right away."

She walked, or rather flounced, out. I didn't know much about girls but I sensed that she was a bit of alright.

After washing and dressing, I went down the hall to where Madeleine's room was. The hallway walls were hung with prints of a variety of subjects, but the one that fascinated me was entitled "The Dance of the Dervishes." It depicted a group of Arabs dancing around a fire, watched by a larger crowd in the background. The postures were exaggerated and grotesque, and their expressions fierce and distorted. The firelight threw their facial characteristics into violent relief; they all had daggers or swords in their hands and one of them stared out of the picture with a look of such hatred and contempt, that it made my flesh creep. He seemed to be looking at me, and I was never able to pass that picture without starting to run to get by in a hurry, especially at night when the dim lighting of the hallway seemed to emphasize the horror of the scene.

I collected Madeleine and we went down to breakfast.

The dining room was large with a high ceiling. Along one wall, a mahogany dresser was laid with hot dishes, steaming pots, and layers of plates kept warm over a spirit stove. The opposite wall was divided by two French windows that led out to a gravel drive, on the other side of which were lawns and flower beds. The rest of the walls were hung with oil paintings in which serious-looking men and women stood in stiff attitudes, usually with horses in the background being held by grooms. Some of the men were in uniforms of the 18th century, though one of them wore half-armour and the long wavy hair of the time of the Restoration.

Grandfather was sitting at the head of the table.

"Good morning. Did you sleep well?"

"Thank you Grandad, very well," I answered.

"Help yourself to breakfast," he said.

I turned to the buffet. Laid before us: porridge, eggs (boiled scrambled, poached, and fried), bacon and cold ham, kedgeree (which is a mixture of rice, fish, and eggs), liver and kidney, grilled tomatoes, and grilled kippers. Little containers with marmalade, plum jam, raspberry and strawberry, apricot, and red current, together with racks of hot toast, were arrayed in echelon along the broad polished table, rather in the fashion of maps one sees in military manuals depicting regiments attacking forts and earthworks, coloured red, green, and purple. Bustling around with plates and cups were the two maids we had already met.

Grandad's place at the table was surrounded like a strong point, defended by tins of various medications and specialized health foods. He was apparently always trying some new additive or patent medicine. Out of the corner of my eye, as I ate spoonfuls of hot, creamy, sugary, porridge, I noticed some of the items. Sanatogen a nerve food, a small bottle of glucose, some metal containers with medical prescriptions on them, together with a row of small pill boxes in the outer works.

He very carefully measured out portions, meticulously screwing on caps and placing the article back into its designated position in the collection. It was as if he were conducting some form of obscure religious ritual in which the administration and mixing of certain potions and cereals was an important and integral part. This illusion was heightened by a habit he had of, after every sampling, closing his eyes, puckering his lips, and placing his hands together in an attitude of prayer. I thought of the Jaffa oranges.

Madeleine and I tucked into the food and I was just spreading marmalade on my second piece of toast when Constance came into the room followed by a small boy, who in turn was followed by a middle-aged woman with her arms full of books and papers. This must be James and his Nanny.

"Teddy and Madeleine, I want you to meet James. And this is Miss Blackett, James' Nurse."

"How do you do?" we all said, almost in unison.

"Don't get up. I've already had my breakfast hours ago."

It was then eight-fifteen. I was to learn that Constance was a compulsive cleaner and tidier, and would get up every morning at six with the servants, put scarf on head, and vacuum and dust with the maids. She continued, "and James and Miss Blackett have eaten in the nursery."

I wondered then who all this food was for. Grandad had his own peculiar diet and only went up to the dresser for a helping of brown sugar for his creamed wheat. I then noticed the maids taking almost all the uneaten and indeed untouched food back into the pantry. I realised that this would all be consumed in the kitchen. They ate after we had finished. Considering the quality of the food, and the quantity, they didn't do badly at all.

James was an unusual boy. He was Constance's child by Percy, a not unexceptional feat when one considers the age of my Grandfather. James being about six at this time, would put Grandad's age at sixty-five at time of conception. Perhaps there was something in those health foods after all.

James was a thin, pale child, with a head that seemed too large for his body. Very quiet, he only spoke when addressed, and then in a voice so low that it was hardly audible. His eyes were large and mournful. His ears, also on the big side, stuck out on either side of this head, giving him the unfortunate appearance of a sad little gnome. He was, by relation, our uncle.

After breakfast we all followed Grandad into the study. We were to hear the ten or eleven o'clock news. He did not yet possess a wireless set, but had an old-fashioned crystal set which was fitted with earphones. To enable others to listen, these were placed onto an earthen-ware pudding basin and the sound would be radiated weakly into the room.

We all sat round while Grandad fiddled with the knobs. James sat with eyes downcast. Miss Blackett, back straight, feet firmly placed on the floor, looked around at us. Her expression seemed to indicate that we were about to hear some sort of admonition, and further, that it was fully deserved. With her hair coiled up on either side of her head, and her mannish facial characteristics (including a distinctly hairy upper lip), she looked for all the world like a radio operator with ear-set in position.

Very faintly we heard the announcer introduce Mr. Chamberlain, then Prime Minister. We listened, only half understanding the sense of what was being said, until towards the end when he told us that we were at war with Germany. When the tired, thin voice ended, we all sat and looked at each other. It was the first time James had looked directly at me. He gave me a nice smile.

We explored Haddiscoe Hall and environs many times during our stay. It was a Georgian structure built of grey brick, with the typical sets of windows arranged symmetrically, handsome white painted door, the walls part ivy-covered, the roof blue-black slate with a low rake. The back of the house was a fair bit older, a soft rosy red. No symmetry here. A comfortable hodgepodge of angles and corners, dormer windows and lunettes. The main part was attached to lower outhouses that meandered back towards more buildings in the rear: stables, barns, and greenhouses. This was Larcombe's territory.

I was to meet Larcombe under unfortunate circumstances. I had wandered alone into the kitchen garden, which happened to have high brick walls around it. On the walls, in certain areas, were espaliered trees: pear, peach, and fig. I was helping myself to a second fig when I heard a hoarse, and definitely unfriendly shout.

"Ere, what d'yer think yer doin?"

I looked around. A man stood there with a spade in one hand and the other raised, as if to shade his eyes from the sun.

"Well, I'm having a fig. Is it forbidden?"

"Oh, are you be young Mast' Teddy from Lunnon, I reckon."

"Yes that's right. Who are you?"

"I'm Larcombe, head gardener for the Major." I never did find out his first name, though I think it was George.

"He'll tan you if he knows you been eatin' his prize figs."

"Well, don't tell him, will you?"

He grunted, grinned, and laid his forefinger on his lips. This was the first of many secret pacts made with this changeable man.

After his initial grumpiness, he became almost friendly and as we walked around the garden, he was inclined to chat. As we moved from clump of parsley to bed of asparagus, he told me about the season they had had. The crops of sugar beet, the prevalence of greenfly in the roses that year, the incidence of Colorado beetle in the spuds, and the extraordinary attacks of starlings on the fruit trees that spring.

He was a tall spare man, his face a bright brick red colour ending abruptly and changing to white at the collar line. He had bright blue eyes that were always wrinkled, as if in protest against the light. His teeth were brilliantly white and straight. He wore (and I never saw him in any other kind of dress), a soiled tweed cap, square on his head, an old frayed flannel shirt taken in at the neck with a brass stud, no collar, just a red bandana kerchief tied there, a waistcoat without buttons, and corduroy trousers held up by braces tucked into a disreputable pair of rubber Wellington boots. It was a lovely outfit and I couldn't wait to get one just like it.

If Larcombe taught me all about fruit trees, how to tell a manged wurzel from a turnip, a Jerusalem artichoke from a parsnip, how to dig and spade properly, how to identify myriad pest and plant diseases and when was the proper time to pot, plant, manure, hoe, weed, spray, and reap, Beaver taught me field craft. Beaver was my grandfather's gamekeeper.

Apparently there was good shooting throughout the acreage that Grandad owned, and the frequency of poaching was such as to require the services of a full-time sentry, for that, in effect, was what Beaver was. He also had a young lad, not much older than me, but a good deal more clever, as his assistant. This was Sam.

Beaver was an exceedingly friendly, stout man, who always smelled slightly of cloves and rum. He had little beady brow eyes, and a shiny, round face. His chin was covered with stubble. I noticed that this bristly hairiness never got any longer or shorter, leading me to wonder if some sort of stoppage of growth had occurred. The hair on his head (if any existed, for I never saw it) was invariably hidden by a rat catcher's cap pulled tight and low down on his forehead. His teeth, which he showed a lot, were large and protruding, giving him for all the world the look of an ingratiating otter. The name was fitting.

On pearly grey, early misty mornings, hands numb with cold, trying not to sneeze or otherwise give my position away, I would stand behind a tree waiting for Beaver to walk up with some pheasants or grouse, the dogs, Bo and Oscar, quivering at my feet. Both black Labs, they were talented field dogs, although Bo had a bad tendency to break and run towards the target too early, a habit that was to lead to a tragedy later.

I had access to Grandad's gun room, my favourite room in the house. It was paneled in light pine with racing and hunting prints around the walls. Tall glass and wood cabinets held the guns. These consisted of handmade shot guns and rifles, covering almost every calibre and type then available. Other walls were lined with low, glass-fronted bookcases. In the middle of the room there stood a large and handsome library table covered with a green baize cloth. It was the repository for stacks of neatly piled periodicals and cartons of cartridges. A lamp stood on it casting a mellow light overall. Its drawers held more small heavy packages of bullets and equipment for cleaning guns. In one corner of the room stood a chest-high wooden cabinet with narrow brass-rimmed drawers. This contained Grandad's butterfly and insect collection. Although I was allowed to use most of the guns, except the bigger, heavier ones like the duck guns, I preferred a nice handy little four-ten that I had become quite a good shot with.

I used to spend a lot of time alone wandering about the fields and woods that surrounded the house. A path led from the front of the building through an iron gate set in a crenelated wall that was said to be the remains of a Norman keep. It meandered downhill through heavy woods of beech and oak. The leaves were heavy on the ground now and the air felt damp.

Following the path, which now paralleled the banks of a small shallow stream, I came upon a large lake, in the middle of which stood a small island with a miniature house on it. I then noticed beyond the island, swimming blissfully about, several dozen geese, swans, ducks, and other species of waterfowl.

The path followed the edge of the water, on the banks of which, at one part, was built a small boathouse and dock. Moored to the dock was a punt and dinghy. Further on were some high bushes of rhododendron, thick with dark shiny green leaves.

Over time our routine was established. We would

get up at seven, have breakfast, read the papers, spend an hour with James in the nursery, at which times we would do a little work on studies set the night before by Grandad, then lunch, followed by a walk with the dogs. Madeleine and I would sit in the library with the wonderful books there.

Then came time for tea, which was an enormous meal. One of the maids would start serving at four. She would be in afternoon uniform, black and white after lunch. After everything had been placed on the table, another maid would enter and help Constance in the serving, pouring, and slicing.

After tea there were more walks, more reading, and then the news on the wireless. Grandad and Constance would have a glass of sherry, then dinner would be announced and we would all troop back into the dining room. Afterwards, Grandad would read, Constance would sew or write and we would play upstairs with James until bedtime. We would then go in and kiss Constance and Grandad goodnight, and start up the stairs to the bedrooms.

We were to be visited by Mummy and Daddy one weekend. They had, in one of their infrequent letters, told us to expect them Friday evening on the six, o'clock train. Auntie Constance was going to meet them at Beccles and we were to be allowed to stay up a little later as a special treat. We hadn't seen our parents for six months, so when the car rustled up to the front door we were terribly excited and rushed outside. The doors opened and Mummy got out. Daddy appeared from the other side. We both tried to hug and kiss Mummy at the same time, laughing and crying, talking a mile a minute. Daddy gave me a quick squeeze and offered a dry smooth cheek to kiss. We all went towards the front door, hand in hand.

"We hope you both have been good children," said Mummy.

We answered that we had, for other than the time I had rather unwisely left some bath taps running and almost flooded the back of the house, and had mistakenly shot a heron, a heavily protected bird, I had behaved. Madeleine, on the other hand, would not allow the enforced, isolated country living to minimize her social life and was inclined to secret visits to the village after dark. I was in on this but I wasn't quite sure what it was that she did when she got there. I suppose it had something to do with holding hands and kissing, which to me at that time of life, constituted the very essence of daring and illicit sin.

Madeleine had, even then, begun to show a tendency toward rebelliousness that caused people to view her in a less favourable light. This attitude was especially directed at persons who were to have a hand in trying to direct her life, and specifically aimed at those of her family. She preferred the company of those considered by her authority figures to be inferior in education and social standing.

The visits to the lads of the village were as often as not made in the company of one of the maids. She was always on the best possible terms with all the help in the kitchen. I had always envied her intransigent personality, for I was utterly without even the smallest degree of combativeness, and, desiring a quiet life at all times, sought, in what I considered an agreeable manner, the peaceful pursuits of a country schoolboy.

This was the period of what was subsequently to be called the "Phoney War." Nothing very frightening had happened; neither side showed the slightest degree of aggressiveness or pugnacity. There had been some shooting and loss of life at sea, and a rabbit had been killed by a bomb dropped by a fleeing Dornier jettisoning his load due to inclement weather over Scotland. Otherwise, things seemed quite normal.

We were to return to live in London. It seemed that father was to join his regiment in Scotland and would accompany us home to stay for only a short time before he was to leave us again. We were to travel next morning.

Constance left no doubt in anyone's mind as to her relief at this plan. Grandad seemed less pleased, and in fact voiced his opinion rather strongly. He thought the decision to go back to town exceedingly unwise. He felt that this quiet period of the war was purely the calm before the storm. The events that followed were to prove him correct.

We said our goodbyes tearfully. We had been quite happy for those few months. James and I had become good friends and he looked particularly sad as we shook hands.

We went to the back of the house and said our

farewells to the staff. Larcombe grunted and looked away. Mrs. Beaver wept openly, dabbing her pink face with her apron. All the other girls hugged Madeleine and fled into the kitchen. Constance stood in the background frowning.

"Well, goodbye dear boy." Grandad pressed my hand with his.

"Hooray!" I felt some coins, two half crowns by the shape and weight.

"Goodbye Grandad. Thanks so much!"

Madeleine was treated to the same embrace and distribution of pocket money. We all got into the car and drove away.

Looking back through the rear window I could see Grandad standing, waving his cap. Next to him, the diminutive figure of James.

The train for London was standing waiting to leave when we got to the station, so there was no time for prolonged leave-taking, much to everyone's relief. Except for a quick cheek to cheek, the transition from platform to compartment was brief. I noticed, as the train gave a warning hoot, that Constance did not wait and wave, but was already out of sight, gone to the car, before the train had even begun to move.

"Oh, I say, I do think that's a bit thick," Father said. "Well I'm sorry sir, but I'm afraid I shall have to insist." The large and florid policeman and Daddy were having argument about the blackout arrangements. My father, not being the most practical or handy sort of man, had erected a travesty of a screen, and the constable was engaged in a critique of a technical nature.

The construction under discussion was finally assembled to the satisfaction of the officer, who was now freely perspiring and had removed his helmet, revealing a pale receding forehead. Father had long given up the struggle and had retreated to his study to brood on the intricacies of air raid precautions, leaving the question of tape versus tacks, and black paper as opposed to black cloth, to my mother to decide upon. Paradoxically, Mother, who appeared to be the most impractical of persons, was to prove herself to be quite competent in the trials that were to follow.

The week ended with a bang. There had obviously been a hell of a good send-off party for my father. Everyone from the Rosslyn Arms, the Duke of Brunswick, the King William and the George, had gone to Euston Station, and, as we heard, carried Dad shoulder high to his carriage. They addressed him, as everyone did then, as Colonel, even though he was in fact only a second lieutenant in the reserve. This was in the presence of two elderly Majors, who with some alacrity, made room for Dad, helping him with his luggage. As he was still in civilian clothes at the time, the misunderstanding continued throughout the trip. We learned later, he was treated with this deference all the way to Scotland. I doubt if my father spent more uneasy hours than those on the Flying Scot that day.

Back at Thurlow Road, we plunged back into our struggle with recalcitrant window and door screens, ration books, stirrup pumps, and sand buckets. Although we had all been issued gas masks, no one by this time thought that they would ever be used, and most people carried sandwiches or, in some cases, make-up apparatus in them, but certainly not respirators. One had to carry them, as one would be subject to a fine if stopped by a policeman when gasmaskless. So they became objects of unintended practicality.

It was about seven thirty in the evening when the siren wailed its warning. We had all been through the daylight raids and watched the Battle of Britain take place over our heads. We had gone to the top of Parliament Hill and seen the southern horizon in flames, the docks and the east end burning. Nothing too serious had occurred in our immediate vicinity however, and we were beginning to think that the blitz might pass Hampstead by. We were about to receive our baptism by fire.

The siren had no sooner ended its mournful message, as we were huddled apprehensively in the coal cellar, when the first droning sound of airplane engines came into earshot. One could always tell unfriendlies from one's own, by the unsynchronised note of the German planes, ominous and foreboding. The uh-uh-uh-uh of the motors followed by the sharp crack, crack, of the anti-aircraft guns.

Closer and closer the noises came until it seemed as though the whole house was shaking. Then as the airplanes rumbling overhead seemed poised right over our street, I felt as though all the bomb-aimers were concentrated on our house. The first terrifying sound of a bomb coming down emerged from the cacophony around us.

It started as a high pitched whistle that got louder and louder until the whistle thickened into a roaring, and sound became movement as the house began to wave and undulate in tune to the all-enveloping falling thunder. The crash, as it exploded somewhere, was something of an anticlimax, sounding somewhat innocuous and deflated. It had, in fact, landed several streets away and had never posed a threat to our safety. We, however, were reduced to a state bordering on hysteria.

Mummy was an absolute brick throughout this and later similar ordeals, and we were strengthened and encouraged by the example she set. Little did we know then the horrors of the lonely desperation she was hiding from us: the miseries of constant ill health and fears of the unknown that were made worse by the lack of news from Daddy, and the overpowering feeling that she must have been experiencing of having been completely abandoned by him.

The winter, with its miseries, had come and gone. The bombing continued unmercifully. One could set one's watch by the punctual evening visits of the raiders. Mummy seemed to become more withdrawn with every raid, and it was obvious that the nightly strain was beginning to take its toll on her constitution, never robust at the best of times. We had received one letter from Father saying that he hoped to get us up there away from the bombing, but week passed into week, and no good news came.

Finally one awful night, we had gone to the shelter under a shop on the high street, and, after the usual noisy night, had been ejected by the warden, for at that time it was the policy to clear all the public shelters out at the end of a raid. It was about three o'clock and very cold. Mummy was sick and we had to support her home. She went to bed at once.

"I'm afraid your mother is very ill," Dr. Nicholson, our family doctor, said. He zipped up his bag and took off his glasses. He blew on them and wiped them briskly with a white handkerchief which he took out of his sleeve.

"She should really go to Hampstead General, but the beds are full with the air raid casualties."

"We are hoping to go to Scotland soon to join our father," I said, more in hope than anticipation, not having had any further word from Daddy on this subject.

"Well that would be splendid if it can be arranged.

In the meantime here is a prescription you should have filled."

I immediately wrote to Daddy, telling him what had happened and to my surprise got an answer almost at once. He told us to prepare to come up to Scotland within the next few days, so long as Mummy was able to travel. She perked up a little at the news from Daddy and at the prospect of getting away from the constant anxiety and worry of the blitz. She announced that she thought she would feel well enough to travel in a couple of days. Looking back, I'm sure she wasn't at all well enough to travel, but I didn't ponder the subject further.

The night before we were to leave, we had a very bad raid. The bombers arrived at their usual time, and the banging and whistling began. It was, I was beginning to think, the end of the story. It just seemed so final, the bombs crashing down, the shells exploding fitfully, the glare of the fires. It all seemed so elemental, savage, and out of control. I felt that we would never get to Scotland and safety. It was the worst raid of the war. We were to hear grownups talking about it after.

The next morning the taxi arrived, an ancient Beardmore taxi, driven by an even older-looking chauffeur. We loaded our luggage onto the cab and grumblingly the driver strapped it in quickly. As we drove down Thurlow Road, I was afraid that we would never see Hampstead again.

Dawn was breaking as we entered the Euston Road and began to head for the station. The streets were choked with rubble and debris and it was with difficulty that the driver navigated his way around the obstacles. It took twice as long as normal because of the wreckage across many of the roads, forcing the taxi driver to make several complicated detours. When we finally arrived at Euston, we had only a short time to get our tickets and find the right platform and get a seat.

At about the time we were passing through the gate showing our tickets to the collector there, the sirens began to sound again. I couldn't believe it.

"Oh, Mummy, we'll never make it." Madeleine was in tears.

"Now, now, darlings, it won't be long now. Just be good and don't worry."

I often thought afterwards that all that seemed to matter in those days was to be good. We got onto the train, only to turfed off almost immediately.

"It's the air raid, you know. We can't have people on the train while the raid is in progress. It's the rules."

So there we sat on our suitcases on the platform. Me with my hamper containing my precious Hornby train set, Madeleine looking forlorn, and Mummy fretful and pale, undoubtedly wondering why she had ever left Italy.

The main line station in London had huge curving roofs of iron and glass, and to ensure that the latter did not go in shards every time a bomb landed anywhere near, the enormous plates had been removed. The result was that one could see the sky and what was going on in the sky quite clearly.

The pale blue was criss-crossed with whitish grey contrails spattered with black and white and brown blobs.

These last were the anti-aircraft bursts. The noise was faint as the explosions occurred up high. The batteries firing were some way off and the bang of the guns was indistinguishable. Occasionally, one could hear the rattle of machine gun fire from the aircraft themselves, and now and again a silver flash would give away the position of the planes. Thank God it was only a hit-and-run affair, and as the breeze blew away the smoke, and the sound of the engines and gunfire grew fainter, we began to collect ourselves and prepared to make a dive for the carriages for a decent seat. Facing the engine for me, and the opposite for Mummy who got motion sick very easily.

The "all clear" sounded and the guards and porters began unlocking the doors and allowing passengers on. The train had been crowded and we had shared our chilly, stiff, and cramped adventure on the platform with several hundred other people. Everyone began to return to the train, all as calm as can be. No fuss, no pushing or shoving. I cannot help thinking, on reflection, about how totally unflappable most Londoners were all through those trying times.

Although I was tremendously excited and elated that London and its dangers lay behind us, and the imagined delights of Scotland lay ahead, I could not help noticing that Mummy seemed very sad and put out. She snapped at everything we said, and most of the trip was spent in gloomy silence. In retrospect, the strains and frustrations of the last few months, combined with the uncertainty of the future, were probably making her even more irritable than ever. Perhaps the new life in the north would do her good.

The long journey finally came to an end. We had changed trains at Carlisle, on the border, and were now in a local train that stopped at every halt in Galloway. We were heading for a town on the coast of Ayrshire called Stranraer. I had looked at the map before we left London and had pictured it many times as I lay in bed just before going to sleep. A little harbour, grey steely water, hills behind the town, dark green shadowy firs and pines climbing to the summits, the houses at the foot, white-washed with red roofs. The pleasant, winding, cobbled, streets thronged with burly, hairy, red-haired, men in kilts with bustling fishwives shawled and tartaned, crying their wares from barrows containing, perhaps, baskets of herring and heather. Lots of porridge would be eaten at rustic cottages. Naturally this would be washed down with copious draughts of strong ale and whiskey. I was wrong in almost every detail.

The town was much larger than I had imagined. It did, in fact, lay nested at the end of an almost land-locked bay, and surrounding were tree-covered hills. Otherwise it bore little resemblance to the picture I had painted in my mind.

My father was the Embarkation Staff Officer of the port. He had been promoted to the rank of Staff Captain and so was entitled to wear an imposing armband of black and red, superimposed with the Royal Coat of Arms, as well as having a large khaki-coloured Humber car, complete with a saluting, door-opening, corporal chauffeur. It was all exceedingly grand and I was very impressed.

We drove through the busy street crowded with traffic mostly of a military variety. Stranraer, I found out, was a principal port for Northern Ireland, and there was a constant flow of troops and equipment back and forth across the Irish Sea, and consequently in and out of the town. All the people looked, to my disappointment, very ordinary, just like us. I don't think I saw a kilt, except on some soldiers of a Scottish regiment, and they were probably from Birmingham or Manchester.

We pulled up in front of a large hotel and a porter ran down the steps to open the car doors and carry our stuff inside. Daddy, with Mummy on his arm – she seemed completely recovered and gazed at Father adoringly – led the way.

The name of the hotel was "The George." It was one of those old-fashioned spa-type establishments that still dot Scotland, very comfortable and substantial. The food reminded us of Haddiscoe, only with the emphasis on fish. We had fish for breakfast, for lunch, for tea, and for supper. We had kippers and herring, cod, hake, and sole. There would be fish paste sandwiches at tea time, "Finnan Haddie" or salmon for dinner, preceded often by a shrimp cocktail or a dozen oysters.

We had a large room that overlooked the town, the hotel being situated halfway up a steep road that continued past the grounds, to disappear over the top of the hill. Daddy had to sleep most of the time in his own quarters at the docks. He would join us often at tea time and supper time, but more often than not left right after the meal.

Large convoys were moving at that time and he was kept fully occupied at his office.

Madeleine and I spent many happy days here. We made lots of friends at the hotel, children of other military, naval, and air force personnel. I was allowed onto the long pier that stretched into the central harbour, and spent hours watching the activities that went on both amongst the marching soldiers on land, and the movement of all the ships and light craft on the water. The weather was often misty and hazy and lent an air of mystery and suspense to the scene. A large troopship, pushed and pulled by tugs, would emerge from the fog hooting mournfully, with a destroyer, siren blipping casually, threading its way through the traffic.

There were several young officers around the hotel, especially navy types. Apparently part of the building housed a branch of naval intelligence. Whatever it was, there were a lot of very young sub-lieutenants running around. Some of them already paying attention to my sister, true to form. She showed not the slightest interest in them, and, much to Daddy's chagrin, took up with his chauffeur.

The remainder of the summer went by quietly. It was very peaceful up there and Mummy seemed to gain strength and good spirits.

It was a great shock, therefore, to come home from a walk one day to find an ambulance outside the hotel, surrounded by a group of people. Amongst them was the figure of Daddy. He saw us and at once beckoned us over. To our horror, we saw that they were gently putting a stretcher with Mummy on it into the ambulance. She was unconscious and looked very pale.

"Your mother's very seriously ill."

"What's wrong with her?" I asked.

"Exhaustion, worry, and physical strain. Her limit of endurance has been reached and she just collapsed."

I had lately been obsessed with the matter of impermanency. I believe, at that moment, as the ambulance drove away with Mummy in it, that I had my first pangs of apprehension about the finality of life.

We went to the hospital every day and sometimes several times a day, and although Mummy at first seemed to respond to treatment, it was not an optimistic report that the doctor gave us.

Madeleine and I had gone for a walk. It had been blustery and raining all day and just after tea a fitful sun had come out, so having been in the stuffy room since breakfast, we decided to put raincoats and galoshes on and get some fresh air. We had walked for about an hour and as it was getting dark now, we started to head back. Our walk took us past the hospital and we thought we might stop in and see if there had been any improvement in her condition since we had been there yesterday.

"Isn't that Daddy's car?" Madeleine asked. It was. I recognised the Corps or Divisional markings on the front fender.

It struck me as strange at the time that the car was parked outside the main entrance. I knew that something was terribly wrong. Madeleine must have been seized with the same idea, as she took off at a turn and was halfway up the steps before I could move.

When I finally got to the front door I blundered into the figure of Corporal Wheeler, Daddy's batman.

"I'm afraid I've got bad news. Your mother is awful poorly. The Captain's asked me to find you and bring you here." I nodded blindly.

"Yes, we were going for a walk and thought we'd visit."

"That's right, you 'op in there and we'll find you a nice hot cup of tea afterwards."

I hesitantly went towards the entrance of Mummy's room. As I was about to turn the door handle, it was wrenched open from the other side and Madeleine came out, her face tear stained. She was weeping uncontrollably. She looked at me unseeingly, and pushing past me, ran up the corridor.

I walked in rather unsteadily. Daddy was sitting by the bed with his head bent. The doctor and a couple of nurses stood in a group in the corner of the room. The curtains were drawn, and except for a light from a small lamp by the bed, the room was in darkness.

I stood uncertainly near the bed and forced myself to look at the figure lying there. Mummy was breathing with difficulty, her face the colour of parchment. Her cheeks had sunk in and perspiration ran off her forehead. A nurse leaned over and wiped her face with a cloth.

I don't know what I said or exactly what I did. It all seemed like some awful nightmare. I couldn't believe that I was face to face with the possibility of death and that the unthinkable was happening. How we had always taken her for granted, how she had always been near when needed!

Her never-ending kindness and sympathy, her affectionate undemanding nature. How everyone always said, "Irene's loved by all, without exception."

It wasn't fair. It wasn't right. It was such a terrible waste. What were we to do without her? How would we cope? Daddy never cared particularly about us. It was always our mother who guided us, washed us, fed us, and cared when we hurt. I tried to think of her feelings, her suffering, her misery, but all I could think about was what we would do without her, and how we would miss her.

I kissed her and she opened her eyes for a second. I'm sure she recognised me. She whispered through dry, cracked lips, some words. I bent closer to hear.

"I'm sorry," she said. I looked at her eyes. She was crying. It was the last I saw of her. She died that night. She was thirty-nine years old.

The next few days passed in a sort of tear-stained daze. We had been sent to stay with friends of Daddy's who had children of our age. They paid lots of attention to us, and gradually the wounds healed and we began to feel better, and other than the sadness at night when alone with that emptiness of loss, we became again, average children thinking mostly of ourselves.

The question of what to do with us on a semi-permanent basis was uppermost in Daddy's mind. He was to be transferred to the Middle East and had to make arrangements for our care and schooling. As far as the latter was concerned, it had been sadly lacking since being evacuated from London in the autumn of nineteen thirty-nine. It was now October nineteen forty-one. Other than some private tutors that had come and gone over the last few months, trying to keep some semblance of education going, we had no formal education of any kind for almost two years.

We found, to our dismay, that he had decided, against the wishes of Auntie Constance, to return us to Haddiscoe. Everyone had come to see us off. We both felt saddened at the prospect of being under the unkind wing of our step-grandmother again, but, as the train rambled through the lovely green hills of southern Scotland, our spirits began to rise. I would see James again and Madeleine was looking forward to renewing romantic acquaintances in the village.

The journey though seemingly interminable, was uneventful, except for losing my stamp collection in Newcastle Station during an air raid. I had been looking at it in a waiting room when the siren sounded and in the confusion I had left it on the seat and gone to the shelter. When we returned it was gone. I was most upset and never completely forgave the Germans.

It was late at night when we finally got to Beccles. Constance was waiting just like before, only this time she looked grimmer. We trembled.

"Hallo Auntie Constance," we said in unison.

"Hallo indeed! I hope you know how very

inconvenient your visit is at this time." It was almost word for word the same welcome she had given us two years ago and probably from her point of view the very pinnacle of understatement. We were, without question, a source of irritation and generally a bloody nuisance to her. We interfered in her life and her routine. She probably considered me a bad influence on James, and what she thought of Madeleine and her inclinations, one could only surmise by the expression of odium on her face when she looked at my sister. I viewed our immediate prospects with some disquiet.

It was almost midnight when we got to the house. Everyone had gone to bed and Constance packed us off to our rooms hungry. No Ovaltine and biscuits this time. As I passed the picture of the dancing dervishes and saw again that baleful stare, I shivered.

The return to Haddiscoe filled me with the utmost gloom. The circumstances were less attractive than they had been two years ago when we had been welcomed, after a fashion, as possible short-term lodgers, or at worst as temporary refugees. Now it seemed highly probable that we might be residents for the duration. The war situation had worsened, and, what in the autumn of thirty-nine had seemed a short and perhaps gentlemanly scuffle of dropped leaflets and rude songs about the washing of the Siegfried line, had now become a murderous conflict that threatened to go on until all combatants were lying dead or exhausted with the world in ruins around them.

As usual, Constance kept up a running commentary on the ineptness of the servants, their lack of skills, their insubordination and general uselessness. To this she was now to add her thinly veiled comments as to our lethargy, gluttony, and choice of religion. We were constantly being told to go out for a walk, exhorted to be less pig-like in our appetites and criticized for our religious learnings. We found the latter hard to swallow as neither Madeleine nor I were particularly devout and really preferred not to go to mass unless we were forced.

Her constant carping on the subject made us defensive and I found myself ready to come to the defence of the church, especially as we always thought of Mummy as the real Catholic. It seemed an attack on RCs was an attack on my mother.

Constance had recently found a hero and we were to be assailed equally now with the virtues of this odd paragon. Stalin and the Russian people were, in her eyes, the real fighters of the war. Everything that happened in the Anglo-American camp was compared against similar occurrences in Russia, always at the expense of the former. She would use the examples of Russia's food shortages when arguing the case for fewer rations for us.

To add to my disquiet, I was becoming more and more worried about Madeleine. She had been getting more and more restless and depressed and had become withdrawn and secretive. I had my trains and James to pass the time, and I would spend hours with Larcombe and the boys in the fields, working and hunting, but Madeleine only had the girls in the kitchen to talk to. Her trips to the village had come to a sudden stop when Constance found out about them and forbade Madeleine to leave the house after dark. I wondered what was going on in her mind.

Lying in bed early one morning, thinking about breakfast – I was always hungry – I was awakened from my dietary contemplations by the sudden opening of the door. Constance charged in looking wildly around. She was in fight attire: flannel gown and hair curlers concealed by scarves tightly knotted.

"Where the hell's Madeleine?" she shouted.

"What do you mean?" I tried to cover the remains of my previous illicit feast, crumbs of ginger biscuits, hard evidence of my nocturnal pantry raids.

"Don't bother. I know you steal from the pantry. You're a very naughty boy and I'm going to punish you severely, especially if you don't tell me where Madeleine has gone!"

"But honestly, Auntie Constance, I've no idea. Isn't she in her room?"

"You know very well she's not there. You wait until your grandfather hears about this. You'll probably have to go bed tonight without supper. And..." she added darkly, "the pantry door will be locked."

She clomped out of the room, thumping menacingly on the floor.

Breakfast was an icy meal. I had been cross-examined by Grandad and Constance again, and though they were satisfied that I had nothing to do with Madeleine's moonlight flight, they still treated me as though I was an accomplice. Perhaps in supplying pilfered food. They were both convinced that I would come to no good, and Grandad mumbled something about the sooner I was old enough for the army, the better. I succumbed to a feeling of loss as I realised that Madeleine had really gone. Though we were never really close as brother and sister, we respected one anther's peculiar interests and affinities, and observed a kind of uneasy alliance. Now I would not even have this flimsy relationship.

More examinations and interviews took place. All the servants were paraded through Grandad's study. The local police were acquainted with the facts, and investigations were put into effect. I thought all this was silly as it was obvious that my sister had left of her own volition. All her clothes were gone and her bed was made up neatly. We would probably hear from her soon. The facts of the matter finally came out when a tearful maid confessed her part in the incident.

Apparently she had lent money for train tickets and supplied transportation to the station. Madeleine had caught the late train to London, and was no doubt at the moment consuming cream puffs at Lyons Corner House.

We got a card later that week. Madeleine stated baldly that she couldn't stand living at Haddiscoe any longer and had gotten a job at a large London store dressing windows. We were not to worry. Constance remarked that this sort of thing wouldn't happen in Russia. Grandad said nothing, but looked at her as though he wished she were in Siberia.

I found myself spending more time with the outside workers. Grandad had procured a tutor for me, a Mr. Shelby, and I would have to spend three hours every morning with him. Mr. Shelby was, however, more interested in the sherry kept in the buffet in the dining room, and would, when he thought I was sufficiently immersed in my studies, go in there on some pretext, only to return wiping his lips delicately with the handkerchief he always kept in his breast pocket. All in all, I can't say my education was much advanced during this period. Even these spasmodic and reluctant forays to the books were likely to be cancelled or postponed due to his indisposition.

The one useful lesson I learned from Mr. Shelby was how to drive a car. He kept an ancient Jowett coupe in a ramshackle old shed behind his cottage. He never drove it on the roads, but would occasionally motor gently up his drive as far as the gates that led to the highway. At this point he would reverse to the house. He never drove to the Hall, always coming on foot. He felt that even driving on his own lane was too dangerous for me, a beginner, so the lessons were conducted on a flat grass meadow that adjoined his property.

I grew rather fond of old Shelby, as our association continued. He was eccentric, of the old school. He used to remark that the only advice his father had ever given him was that red-haired women were not to be trusted. He totally absent-minded and would sometimes forget who I was altogether or confuse me with someone else. His conversation was often vague and disconnected.

"And how is your grandfather today?" he would ask as though my grandfather's health was the most important matter he could conceive of.

"Fine thank you," I would reply.

Later that year, Sam, Beaver's helper, joined the local Home Guard and was telling us all about the fun and games that occurred during training. Both Beaver and Larcombe decided to join. One of the attractions was that they could get out of the house on a Sunday morning and stop for a quick one at the pub right after drill. I wished that I could go, but, I was too young.

I mentioned this to Grandad that evening, and he said that he would talk to some friends and see if some exception could be made to the age rule. Perhaps I could get in as a cadet or some sort of messenger. It so happened that the commander of the local unit was a good friend of Grandad's, and after seeing how keen I was, and interviewing Grandad, he decided to look the other way when I wrote my age on the application form. I was, after all, tall for my age, and everybody said that I looked at least eighteen.

We all received our uniforms and kit at the same time. We were issued heavy khaki serge battle dress, brown leather gaiters, a forage cap with a brass badge, big black boots, an armlet with the letters "HG" on it, a Canadian Ross rifle of World War I vintage, and five rounds of ammunition.

Mr. Shelby would come to the house every day and we would spend a desultory hour or two on my studies. He did instill in me an interest in English Literature, art, and geography.

The weekends – at least Sundays – were devoted to the Home Guard tactical manoeuvres: mock warfare and enormous fun crawling around, banging off dummy ammo, bayonet drills, and general square bashing, which I was good at. Then we would go to the local pub and drink and boast about what we would do to the German paratroops when they landed.

Nineteen forty-one spiralled to an end. The war was going dreadfully for England and the Japanese had entered the fray with a vengeance, practically wiping out the U.S. fleet in Hawaii, kicking us out of Malaya and Singapore and sinking two precious and prestigious capital ships. The only bright spots were the forced entry of Russia into the war, which effectively brought some relief to huddled thousands in their air raid shelters; and the fact that we now had two allies, albeit reluctant ones, the other being the United States.

Nineteen forty-two came, bringing with it cold dreary days. Still there was bad news from the various war fronts and especially from the battles at sea where it seemed we were rapidly losing the battle of the Atlantic. I knew that was where I wanted to be.

Though I was not yet eighteen, I learned that I was acceptable to the Royal Navy as a boy seaman. To raise money for the train fare to the nearest recruiting office in the city of Norwich I would shoot and skin rabbits and sell the skins for a few shillings. I hadn't told anyone of my plan. I got up very early one morning and walked to the station and caught the early train to town.

" 'Ave a read of that card over yonder," – this from a burly elderly Chief Petty Officer at the recruiting centre. It was the first time that I became aware of my near-sightedness. With horror I realised I could not see any of the letters. Upon blurting this out and seeing the look of exasperation on the Chief's face, and the half-heard comment made by one of the other erstwhile sailors in the office, "the fucker's blind," whereon the Chief said "You're no good to us my boy. Next... " my world was in tatters. I wept openly and found my way back to the station to return to Haddiscoe and whatever awaited me there.

Grandad wasn't upset. In fact, he and Constance were pleased with the initiative I had shown and with my unexpected competence.

A few more months passed, more working in the gardens and fields with Larcombe and Beaver, more studying with Mr. Shelby, who, between sips of sherry and ginger nuts, would endeavour to cram me with the Latin name for the capital of Bulgaria, the whereabouts of the Gulf of Carpentaria and the square root of some incomprehensible figure.

I was delighted when Grandad looked up from The Times one evening, and peering at me over his spectacles asked, "I see that the Navy is taking boys with poor eyesight in certain branches. Do you want to try again?"

My heart leapt. This was it. All the necessary applications were made, the forms completed, and arrangements made. A letter of formal acceptance arrived instructing me to report to the RN recruiting centre at Cambridge.

Young Teddy

Cecil, Lovell, and Zoe Payne

*Percy, Cecil, Lovell
Maude and Zoe Payne*

Haddiscoe

Family at Haddiscoe
Cecil, Constance, Miss Blackett with James in front, Teddy, Irene (Mother)
Madeleine

Joining the line at the old Victorian building that housed the Naval offices, I looked around me. There must have been several hundred young men and boys, all looking excited and anxious. These were all volunteers, and once accepted, would be the property of the admiralty. At one point the line was divided, one section leading to a desk at which sat a naval petty officer, the other ending at a desk at which sat, in all the glory of blue, scarlet, and gold, a sergeant of the Royal Marines trying to gather hopefuls for the commandos.

I lined up for the Royal Marines, imagining the glories we had all heard of. It was my turn at the desk.

"Name."

"Payne Sir."

The pale blue eyes scanned a list of names. "Payne, you're fucking blind. No good to us. Next!"

Back to the other line for the Royal Navy. Now I was looking at the Petty Officer who had witnessed the previous exchange and was now surveying me with barely restrained disgust.

"So, the Navy isn't good enough for you?"

"Oh no Sir, I mean Chief, I mean, yes, er, fine, er..."

"Orl right, orl right. We may not want you. The only jobs left for boys like you are sick bay attendant, officer clerks, and radar."

I weighed the prospects of wiping bums in the sick

bay against the repulsive picture of being an officer's servant and decided on this mysterious radar. I then had a vaguely surreal interview with an elderly lieutenant of personnel who, I noticed, was attended to by a dishy blonde WREN (a member of the British Women's Royal Naval Service). The officer, who had obviously been brought back from retirement, looked up at me.

"Well my boy, how can we help you?"

"Radar, Sir. I am interested, but would like to ask some questions."

A look of alarm spread across his face. "Yes, yes. We'll you'll get all the details at the training camp. It is all about electrically finding the enemy. All very complicated I'm sure. Oh Isabelle, is tea ready yet? Do we have any decent biscuits?" Then back to me, "Oh, are you still here?"

"Yes, Sir. I was wondering, do radar people have to climb masts? I'm frightened of heights."

"Oh, I don't know. I say Isabelle, do radar ratings have climb masts?"

"I don't know, Sir. I don't think so." So radar it was to be.

The Navy bus slowed at the gate and ground heavily to a stop. A sailor in gaiters and webbing equipment, with a large revolver holster attached to his hip, sauntered over, flicked through the pass our driver produced, and waved us through. I looked around with interest. This was to be my home for the next few months.

The HMS Royal Arthur was known in the Navy as a "stone frigate." It was all grey bustles, boats attached with chains in the swimming pools for rowing practice, gun emplacements, real-looking and menacing. Sailors were all around, all shapes and sizes, and I noticed the many girls with great interest. WRENS in the Navy looked so unattainable, but highly desirable in their tight little blue suits and sexy black stockings.

The next few weeks passed in a blur: issue of kit, blue serge, suits, overalls, white ducks, oddly worn when in cells under punishment, caps and underwear and socks, a stiff sort of rubberised outerwear to be worn in foul weather, which, as this camp was on the coast of Lincolnshire, was frequent. Then, in quick succession, shots for every conceivable disease, a fast and brutal visit to the dentist, and we were ready for the parade ground.

Under the malevolent glare of a Chief Gunnery Petty Officer we were introduced to the finer points of forming threes, musket drill, and general all-around rules for repelling an attack by some savage foe. I discovered afterwards that the Chief boasted, among his medal ribbons, one for the attempted relief of Gordon of Khartoum. Although we were to be prepared for a twentieth-century conflict, radar for instance seemed rather ultra and up to date, the basic training was designed as though the foe were to be spear throwers and bearers of swords.

The day we were waiting for finally arrived. We were considered ready for the next level, which was the technical training of the various branches. Before we were sent on our different ways, we were given our first liberty ashore. We were encouraged to speak and behave as though we were already at sea. Off we trotted ashore through the gates we had entered so long ago, and into the town of Skegness.

We wandered about gaping idly at shop windows, steamed up fish and chip shops, and bedraggled dancehalls. We finally opted for one of the local cinemas where we saw Noel Coward taking on the Germans and Celia Johnson in "In Which We Serve."

Suitably chastened we wended our disillusioned way back to the camp. Leave was over at eleven... and wakey wakey... reveille came early.

The next day after breakfast of tinned herrings in tomato sauce known as "herrings in," bread and margarine, and hot, strong, and very sweet tea, we were off. I was being sent to another camp in North Wales at Pwllheli. It was perched on a rocky and scenic part of the coast, very beautiful and strangely bleak: black stony beaches littered with pungently smelling seaweed, long stretches of sheep-cropped grassy headlands upon which we were expected to patrol as part of our training.

We spent the next few months being chased over assault courses, at firing practice with a variety of weapons, drilling on the parade square, and trying to keep awake in muggy classrooms where the intricacies of locating an enemy warship and/or airplane on a tiny blue or green disc-shaped screen were taught. By the end of the summer we were ready for sea.

We entrained at the little railway halt of Pen-y-chain and spent seemingly endless dry and hungry hours until we detrained at Crewe. Probably every man or woman who served in any service during the war changed at Crewe.

The Church of Scotland had the best free canteen. You could get beans on toast, fruit cake, tea, and a packet of cigarettes, a smile, and no lectures or sermons. Then, into a waiting room jammed with snoring bodies with labels on them such as "Wake me for the number three hundred for Edinburgh" or "shake for the troop train for Stranraer" or "for God's sake don't let me miss the train to Cardiff."

My train was a no-corridor slow branch that went by a devious route to the south of Wales, where the ship that I had been assigned to lay. A smoky fog in the compartment lay heavily on those pre-war pictures on the partitioning walls: the stag at bay, sheep being eyed by ratty sheep dogs, and ancient crofters contemplating a damp highland valley. I looked around at my companions, I had a corner seat and was in comparative luxury and comfort. I procured a couple of ham sandwiches and a cup of tepid tea and was in fairly good shape. I also had a full packet of cigarettes, which put me in an even better state of mind.

Opposite me were two RAF types, aircraftmen, with acne and no ambition, and then a private in the Pioneer Corps. On my side was a very angry-looking military policeman hand-cuffed to a scruffy soldier being taken to detention somewhere. Finally, looking as though she hoped the floor would swallow her up, was a nifty looking WREN.

I asked her where she was going. Penarth Dock, which was where my ship was in dock. Her name was Mary and she was from Kent. We shared sandwiches, we cuddled and ate and smoked and the rest of the compartment snoozed in the half light as we chugged through the night.

We must have rattled and clanked through a dozen counties to get from Crewe to Cardiff. Dawn came in some coal valley, blearily seen through gummed-up eyelids, the compartment sounding hollow with smokers, and scratching and the adjustment of clothing.

Dark, cavernous Cardiff Station... the train pulled into a deserted early morning terminal and came to a steaming, blowing, wheezing stop. Doors slammed. Shouting porters grabbed kit bags. Mary gave me a perfunctory kiss in the confusion, ran some lipstick over her mouth, smiled, and disappeared into the crowd.

We struggled with our heavy bags containing all our possessions, and the awkward sausage-shaped hammocks that all British sailors slept in, looking around hopefully for transportation. There was none.

"Alright get fell in. Shortest on the left, tallest on the right. Attention by the right. Quick march. Put that fucking fag out Payne. Left, right, left... ." We swung out of the station yard crisping along on a thin layer of snow, crunch, crunch, watching the dark blue back in front swaying along.

After a while someone played a harmonica and we all sang. An hour later... no singing, and only the weary exchange of curses and the odd whistle. We entered the dockyard gates marching to attention. We straightened in spite of ourselves. We were well trained. The sentry at the gate came to a salute as we swung through the portals.

We passed destroyers, lean and aggressive, steam escaping from frigates, convoy escorts, and corvettes. I was eager to see the ship I had been drafted to.

The Chief in charge yelled out the order to halt in threes, left turn, and stand easy. There, bristling with guns and painted in the most alarming dazzle camouflage – pale grey, white, black and blue – was the Ulster Queen, to be my home for the next year. The Chief made an about turn and trotted briskly up the gangway where he saluted, made another about-turn back down the gangway and barked, "Attention. From the right. Single file. Quick march. Follow that man," as he pointed at a bearded overalled sailor standing on the upper deck. We quickly followed this figure on board.

Crossing the deck was no easy business, there were men everywhere, busy with matters maritime and nautical. There were strange smells, steam mixed with diesel oil fumes, cooking and acrid electric smells, tarred ropes, and myriad scents of a busy harbour. It was lovely.

We found our quarters, which were in the most forward part of the ship – nothing between us and the bow but the anchor cable compartment and the cells. We were just at the waterline, in a steel room shaped like an oblong box with slanting sides in the shape of the hull.

We settled quite quickly, and after a few days started to feel more at home. We slipped into a routine: learning, working, scrubbing, eating, sleeping, and taking shore leave for the days to come. The food was plain but wholesome and there was plenty of it. We were given one real egg per week, oranges – not seen at home for years – and a rum ration distributed daily. I was too young, but everyone in the mess gave me a bit of their tot so afternoons were spent rather cheerfully. On top of these luxuries were duty-free cigarettes, big fat Virginias with "HM Ships Only" stamped on the sides.

After the working-up period we were subjected to a series of tests given by an elderly commander of the RNVR, who, after a few cock-ups on our part, pronounced us fit for sea. Many of our officers were either RNVR or RNR. This stood for "Royal Navy Voluntary Reserve" and "Royal Navy Reserve," the former, ex-amateur sailors, and the latter ex-merchant mariners. These last were experienced blue water sailors and basically ran things. All the others, including us hostility-only ratings, learned as we went along. It all worked well eventually.

We arrived at Greenoch, at the mouth of the river Clyde, and hove to. With the help of a tug, we tied up at a buoy. I looked around. There were ships of all descriptions moored around us, liners converted to troop ships, the most astounding being the Queen Mary – enormous in grey paint. Others not so well known were being identified by the older salts leaning at the rail near me. They seemed to know them all. Other craft were rusty tramp steamers, oil tankers, large ships and small. Meanwhile the whole scene was dotted with small craft busily scurrying between ships. Overhead aircraft buzzed and hummed, altogether a sight to be savoured.

We were, in turn, loaded with food supplies, fresh water, fuel, and ammunition. Some shore leave was granted, but soon we were off to sea.

One gloomy windy evening we let go all connection with the earth and sailed downriver to join a convoy bound for Halifax, Canada. It seemed to take forever, but finally the ships all found their places and we picked up to our cruising speeds of between seven and ten knots. This was a slow convoy. The Queen Mary was not with us, mostly creaky old tubs making the pace with difficulty, some belching gulps of thick black smoke from their funnels – not a good thing I thought, when invisibility was the desiderata.

When I wasn't on watch, I could hang about on top and take in the sights. I had to work at seamanship duties, which mostly consisted of scrubbing decks and chipping paintwork. We were given plenty of time off to wash clothes and darn socks; otherwise we played cards and bingo and would talk about everything except the war. We slept a lot in bad weather, which in the north Altantic was most of the time. We rarely changed our clothes so the fug below deck was at times almost unbearable. We all wore lifebelts at all times in case of emergency.

I found, to my dismay, that I was a not good sailor, but was able to survive somehow. I could handle medium bad conditions, but when it really blew and steep seas tossed us about, I would creep away and hide in a locker that held spare hammocks. My mates would do watches for me and bring me sandwiches until it calmed down. Some storms lasted for days, so life was not exactly hilarious.

Fortunately, this trip was fairly quiet and eventually ended with us handing the convoy over to the Canadians, who came out to meet us at the mid-ocean point. After much coming and going and flashing of signal lamps, we did an about-turn and headed with the wind, back the way we had come.

The return to England was without incident, the weather behaving until we neared England where it started to get dirty again. By this time though, we were in sight of the coast. I noticed, parenthetically, that the first thing one saw was the Blackpool Tower, an odd reminder that other life was going on in another world.

It was the end of nineteen forty-three. Some of us were given short Christmas leave. I went to London to see, and hopefully to stay, with my father, as he had just been invalided out of the army. He had taken a notable part in the campaign from Madagascar, up the East African plains, through the mountains of Abyssinia, to the town of Asmara in Italian Eritrea. He had unfortunately been stricken by an old nemesis from earlier times, malaria, became very ill, and now was living in more comfortable surroundings in Knightsbridge. I wondered where the money was coming from to afford this address. I would soon discover the source.

I arrived at the quite smart block of flats that he had given as his address. I tapped at the door. It was early in the day and I had come straight from the station, grubby, tired, and hungry. The door was opened at once by a pretty woman in her late thirties. I was also aware of another woman hovering in the background and the smell of frying bacon and coffee in the hall.

"Does Major Payne live here?" I asked.

"You must be Teddy. He certainly does," she said. "I am your new mother."

After the initial shock of this announcement I was told to sit down and made much of. A luxurious bath followed, then breakfast, and then, tucked into bed with clean sheets. I was admonished to rest until lunch when I was to be taken out. I floated into a blissful sleep.

Lunch at a pub on Baker Street was mostly liquid, and other than the fact that my new mother's friends seemed to be mostly senior officers of all three services, most amusing.

Dad turned up from his stay in the hospital and we spent a few hours together. He did not seem the least bit interested in my naval experience. He disapproved of me going into a rival service and the fact that I had not got a commission. Our meeting was not exactly cordial.

I liked my new mother more than I did my father. Her name was Connie and she was serving in the Red Cross. She loved to party, she loved people, and she appeared to adore my father. It was a short leave...

I returned to the Queen to find her buzzing with rumours. We were going to Russia, or to the East, or somewhere in the Atlantic... It turned out that it was Ceylon or India. I was thrilled. We sailed at night out of the Clyde and joined a convoy in the Atlantic.

It took about four or five days to clear Ireland and

zig-zag in a generally southern direction. Rough, cold, gale-like weather followed us, until one day when I awoke, and rubbing sleep-encrusted eyes, looked around to see that we were alone with no other ships in view. The Queen had parted company during the night. The sea was calm and the air warmer. I was off duty, and so, hung around on the upper deck with some other off-duty ratings and sun bathed.

On one of the legs, looking ahead, I saw a faint smudge on the horizon, Africa, and to the left the Rock of Gibraltar. In what seemed like no time at all, we entered the harbour, our pennant number (indicated with flags) snapped at the mizzenmast. We tied up at our designated mooring.

The following morning at dawn, we left, headed to the Suez Canal, where we passed without incident, and were soon navigating the Red Sea. It was becoming insufferably hot and we were warned that sunbathing was not an allowed tropical pastime. We stopped at Aden to refuel and to top up our ammunition.

Crossing the Indian Ocean was uneventful...

We woke one morning to tooting pipes ordering special duty seamen to fall in for entering harbour. I was on duty that day and scurried to my position. We were very close to the port of Bombay. Over the side of the ship I saw water that turned from iridescent green-blue to a muddy brown. This was the effluvia from the mouth of the river on which the city sits, and as we got closer a strong scent of what I later learned belonged to cooking fats and oils enveloped us. It was pleasant and exotic.

Our stay in Bombay was brief. We continued on...

After several rough sailing days we arrived in Ceylon. It was so attractive – a well-husbanded city – much tidier than Bombay, and there seemed to be much less beggary. We had shore leave here and spent it exploring and swimming at the lovely Galle Face beaches and being fed luxuriously.

Our next port was Trincomalee. This was to be our base until the end of the war.

A lot of time was spent working with the RAF at this time. We had been designated a fighter direction ship for the upcoming landings in Burma, and latterly the landings on the West Coast of Malaya, and the landings at Rangoon.

It was in the very early hours of the day that we were steaming at seven knots towards the Rangoon River. It was the beginning of the monsoon season and was raining gently. There was a low-lying mist across the marshland on our port side. Ahead, the river mouth was marked by buoys and there were signal lights flashing. We were surrounded by landing ships and landing craft crammed with troops, equipment, and various other paraphernalia the Tommies needed.

We had just dropped some commandos in an assault boat, all looking very stern, black-faced and grim, armed to the teeth. They soon disappeared. I wondered what had happened to them.

I returned my attention to my set, which selected that precise moment to go on the blink. The radar mechanics were getting hell from our chief. Having nothing else to do, I left my little iron box and leaned against the guard rail that surrounded the Oerlikon gun position. This was manned by a buddy, Jock Matheson, a tough, red-haired Glaswegian who was our best shot. He was preparing to clear the weapon for later action. He had depressed the gun barrel towards the sea surface, which was the procedure for safety purposes, Rounds bounced off the surface, every fifth one a red tracer. *POM POM POM POM ZIP...* . The brilliant red sparks soared away into the sky. Jock turned and grinned at me.

We were now moving up river with banks close on either side. Suddenly, there was a crashing roar as all other ships opened fire on suspected Japanese positions. Seemingly there was no return fire, for which I was grateful. We found out later, talking to the RAF people, that one of the pilots of the squadron that we were vectoring on target had returned to report seeing on the roof of a Rangoon station, large white painted letters saying "extract digit, Japs gone," a message apparently written by POWs. The enemy had fled.

I hoped this would remain a bloodless event; however, at that moment, there was the most enormous bang followed by a grinding tearing metallic sound. The ship swayed violently to port and I was thrown to the deck. Jock, still upright, was hanging on to the trigger guard of the gun.

I was disoriented, wondering how we had been hit. Then above me and moving fast were aircraft careening down our starboard side. We had practically dropped anchor and were at a standstill. The invasion aircraft passed us by and continued to a city now burning furiously in the distance. We sent down divers who reported damage that could only be repaired in dry dock. The nearest was Bombay.

We turned and headed away from the excitement and pointed southwest, into the teeth of an oncoming storm. That night was hell. I realized fate had befallen us as we were all young and keen in that silly way of the young and foolish.

The storm was short and blew itself out by the next evening. We were almost halfway across the Bay of Bengal. I had the last dog-watch and was turning the wheel of the PPI set, which showed the surface of the sea and everything on it. My Chief Petty Officer, Dusty Miller, was just lighting a cigarette and offering me the match when...

"Christ, what the fuck's that?" The match burned his fingers as he was staring at the screen with its revolving bright beam illuminating a bright spot at the extreme edge. "Quick, reverse the aerial."

I did as he ordered, concentrating on the echo that was moving fast in our direction.

"She's big whatever she is," he said. "Report to the bridge."

"Two eight-one radar bridge."

"Bridge here."

"Echo bearing green one hundred and twenty degrees, twenty five miles, moving fast."

I looked at Dusty.

"Probably a cruiser," he growled.

The blip we were looking at was joined by another

on the screen, and then by another and another until there was a large blob with five smaller blips on either side. It was obviously some sort of capital ship accompanied by destroyer escorts and coming up on us quickly. I reported the additional, unwelcome information.

"Blast!" returned the bridge. "Alright, keep an eye on them." We were sure that there were no friendlies in the neighbourhood and we were nervous. We only had four-inch popguns and if this was a Japanese cruiser they could blow us out of the water.

I felt a shudder and surge as we increased speed. Our top rate was fifteen knots, which we soon reached. I sensed a change in direction. We were swinging to port away from our would-be pursuers. As we moved further to the northwest, the blips continued on to the south, ignoring us. Thank Heavens. The echoes disappeared and we resumed our course to Bombay.

We were later told that the ships were escaping Singapore and that thanks to our radar reports, they had been followed and sunk by our destroyers. I was congratulated by the skipper, and sippers of rum all round the mess put me on my back in my hammock in short order.

We arrived safely at Bombay and spent several weeks in dry dock. We had ample shore leave, which I spent with my chums going to swimming pools in the city, having wonderful Indian curries and drinking a lot of beer.

The next operation was the re-conquest of Malaya

with special attention to the recapture of Singapore where we were to take part in the rescue and release of POWs in the notorious Changhi prison. This began with the assembly of a massive landing force at the Port of Madras on the east coast of India.

We left late in the evening, all of the various ships lining up in predetermined order until we were arranged in columns several thousands of feet wide, an enormous rectangle of warships pitching and rolling over an angry sea. Overhead flew aircraft from the carriers in the fleet. We were obviously preparing for a hot reception. We had been advised not to be taken prisoner by the Japanese.

By the time we reached the coastal area of Malaya, the fleet had been split up. We were now part of a headquarters group and were starting to control fighter cover over the fleet and the defended ground ahead. Smoke was rising from some huts on some small islands in the mouth of the Klang river, which led to the town of Port Swettenham.

Anti-aircraft fire suddenly broke out all along the line of ships. A Japanese Zero fighter screamed down out of the low cloud cover and belted back over the jungle, hotly pursued by two Spitfires and a Fleet Air Arm Corsair, all guns blazing. We cheered as a plume of brown smoke started to stream behind the Zero.

Jock fired a couple of superfluous rounds in the general direction of the fracas and was sternly admonished by Dusty, " 'old your fire Matheson!"

We all laughed. My God, it was exciting. But the anticlimax came with a vengeance.

"Where you going Sparks?" this from Dusty to the telegrapher hurrying forward to the bridge with a flimsy in his hand.

"The war's over! They've dropped some big bomb on the Japanese mainland and the bastards have surrendered." He dashed up on the ladder to the bridge. This was enormous.

"Orl right," said the Chief laconically, "knock off for a five minute smoke."

It took a while to sink in. We had survived after all. Those hopeless forlorn days and nights, the blitz, the breakups and miseries of rationing, my Mum's death. God knows where my Dad was – last heard of in East Africa – and I believed Madeleine to be in America by then. I decided to write to her soon.

I puffed on my cigarette. They were going to splice the mainbrace – a double ration of rum – and a much loved tradition in the Royal Navy. I hastened to the mess.

A few days later, we heard we were to accept the surrender of the garrison at Port Swettenham and when the day arrived, I was part of the watch party. I stood at the top of the gangway. Out from the shore, a short distance from where we tied up at a buoy, came a small steam pinnace. It put-putted alongside our ship, hooked onto the gangway and from beneath the awning that covered the length of the boat, appeared a short, stout, Japanese officer in service khakis and brilliantly shined boots. His brown belt was also shining, and attached to it was a very large sword. He climbed the gangway with a grace and dexterity that belied his appearance, paused briefly, and saluted. He then unbuckled his sword and handed it over. He was crying. Another salute, an about face, and down the ladder into the boat. He undoubtedly took his life that night.

Much time passed... I found myself on a troopship carrying time-expired men from Singapore to Bombay where they went on to England by standard troopships. We then returned either to Singapore or Rangoon and back and forwards we went for the remainder of nineteen forty-five.

This rather boring routine ended when we were told we would go to the Persian Gulf and visit the Port of Muscat in the Trucial Oman, then to the Seychelle Islands, thence to Mombassa in Kenya, to Dar es Salaam and Zanzibar, to the island of Mauritius, to end up in Durban, South Africa. After a short but marvellous visit we continued to the naval base of the South Atlantic fleet at Simonstown, within easy reach of one of my favourite places, Cape Town.

Where Durban was hot and semi-tropical, very modern, with tall blondes everywhere, Cape Town was cooler and more Victorian in appearance, fresher in its air not being that far from the South Pole, but with the common denominator of a generous amount of remarkably beautiful women.

We had wonderful shore leaves. We were swarmed by crowds of people of every description vying to take us to their homes, to lavish hospitality on us. They gave us bed and board, lent us clothes, introduced us to their daughters, unlocked the liquor cabinet, took us to country clubs, theatres, and the beach. Nothing was too good for us it seemed.

However, it soon ended. We found ourselves packing kit bags and hammocks, leaving the ship to take the train to Durban, where we were to sail on the old Orient liner "Orontes" to return to England. Though we were happy to be going home, many were saddened at leaving this paradise on Earth.

Teddy in the Home Guard

Teddy joins the Navy

Teddy's first ship HMS Ulster Queen, A.A. Cruiser, R.N.

Teddy's second ship HMS Jamaica, Crown Colony-Class Cruiser

Teddy (in the middle) on shore leave
Capetown

grass made greener from weeping clouds
burnt brown leaves abound sadly

violet daisies say goodbye as
warm grey blankets cover cold blue sky

fitful shiny brassy beams
light up distant olive hills

clouds passing one by one
in hurry to be gone

night descending wind
rattling bones of trees...

The first of England home and beauty was disconcerting. Misty, with the inevitable drizzle as we came alongside the dock, I saw a sprinkling of people standing about. The gangway went down and an orderly line of soldiers, sailors, and airmen started down to the dock. When I got there, I thought of all that had happened since leaving Penarth so long ago.

Nostalgia soon disappeared when I saw that we were being given packages of sandwiches, cakes, cigarettes and fruit, and cups of steaming hot tea. We all found our places to be: offices where travel warrants to various U.K. destinations were issued. I collected mine.

Down to Norfolk, to see and stay with my grandparents. I had lost touch with my father and had no idea where he was, but hoped to get information as to his whereabouts, and, for that matter, the whereabouts of all the family that had become so spread out during the war. My grandfather and Constance seemed fit and flourishing. Grandad had aged, but was still alert and quite pleased to see me. I had a pleasant visit, then went on to London.

Arriving in London, I made for a hostel I'd been told about. It was situated on a street full of embassies and legations, behind Harrods in Knightsbridge. The place was comfortable and I soon settled and made friends. One of these was John Hammond, who worked for BOAC (British Overseas Airways Corporation) at Heathrow, as an officer in the security department. He at once looked for a job for me. I was already eagerly scanning job vacancies in any paper I could find.

I had decided that I had enough facility to draw and paint and that I might get some sort of job in the advertising business. I signed up for evening classes at Saint Martins School of Art, a locally run school that had a good reputation for turning out skilled, creatively educated people for the commercial art world.

I had no positive results from my enquiries, and study of job ads had so far yielded little, but once again chance played a role in my next adventure. I bumped into an old chum from school days, Alan Fowler. He was working for the United Africa Company and promised to make enquiries at his office. He called me the following week to tell me he had gotten me a job in his firm, but that he had also heard of another company looking for someone like me in their purchasing office. It was a well-known engineering company with offices in the city above Cannon Street Station. The company dealt in heating and cooling systems and power station equipment.

I got an interview with a very likeable man who would turn out to be my future boss. The meeting went well and he promised me another session after he reviewed my qualifications with the board. I heard in a week that I had got the job, assistant to the buyer.

The arrangement did not work however, as I had not enough basic experience in the fundamentals of mechanical engineering. They did find me bright enough to be useful to them later and set me up with a crash course. I went to work in their tool room and learned to operate a centre lathe, a horizontal grinder, a milling machine and do some hand fitting work. They sent me, at night, to a government school three times a week. With my art school studies twice a week, I didn't have much time to play.

Although weekends were hectic too, I found some time, and joined a spiffy little place called the Mandrake in Soho. It was the hangout of art students and pre-dated the hippy movement in all aspects with the exception of drug use. The girls were fun and the decorations clever and bright. We drank our beer and cider and set the world to rights. I was leading a dual life, part mechanical and practical, part artistic and Bohemian.

I managed to locate most of my family. My father worked as an accountant again in the city. Madeleine was happy in America with her family. Aunts and uncles were in Surrey and Dorset farming. Sadly, my Grandfather died, and the arguments over who would get what had started. Surprisingly, I received an insurance policy, which I immediately surrendered for cash. I bought clothes and spent the rest on a big piss-up at the pub for all my chums.

That weekend I had been invited to my Uncle Lovell's, my father's brother's farm, and was looking forward to it. He was my favourite relative and in many ways had supported and influenced me more than my father. He was very handsome, charming, and lively. He could be as generous as he could be funny and was loved by all. He'd had an amazing life up to this point, much of which had been spent in Egypt and Palestine in the oil business, the same line of work my father was in.

Lovell married the daughter of an American family named Spafford, from Chicago. They had migrated to Jerusalem in the late eighteen nineties – a personal pilgrimage following the loss of three infant children in an accident at sea. Subsequently, the heartbroken parents had invested a sizeable sum into the founding and construction of a hospital and home for both Arab and Jewish families.

Lovell also had a proud war-time record and he would talk of his entry into Tobruk hard of the heels of the fleeing Italian army, a story that always amused me. He had apparently taken over his opposite number's office and was sitting at the desk when there was a knock at the door. It was his sergeant major, a red-faced NCO stating: There's a lidy 'ere to see you sir."

"Tell her to come in," said the unflappable Lovell.

The sergeant ushered in a scruffy looking woman of uncertain age, who explained that she was the Madame of the Italian army brothel that had been ungallantly abandoned by the escaping army.

"What can I do for you Signora."

"My ladies, ze haf no clothes."

"But you Signora, have a nice frock."

Yes, but not'ing underneath Colonello," she said, pulling up her dress and revealing the truth.

"Yes yes," said the now perspiring Lovell. "Sergeant, take that smirk off your face and show the ladies the warehouse next door where I am sure they can be accommodated."

Beside this, he organized transport for these 'war time refugees' back to Alexandria, much to the chagrin, no doubt, of the hospital ship's staff. I have recounted the story of Lovell and the Italian prostitutes many times amid gales of laughter.

I arrived at the station at Dorchester to be met by them in an old Land Rover. We laughed and talked, Lovell keeping running commentary on the countryside and its inhabitants, his lovely face animated and happy. Ann, his wife, though friendly and cordial, was now taciturn and given to interjections in Lovell's dissertation.

"You're full of shit, Lovell."

"I am not full of shit my darling Ann," he replied as the both smiled with relish, obviously loving each other to the fullest.

The house they lived in was of considerable antiquity and was quite charming. Set like a jewel in the folds of a sheep-cropped hill, it was the cosiest, most comfortable home I had ever been in. Ann was frequently in the kitchen preparing wonderfully inspired meals, the cooker bubbling and steaming, Lovell hovering ever attentive, with lots of interesting questions and answers on just about every subject. I learned much from my uncle about life, about how to live it fully. He was ever generous, helpful, and empathetic. I know there were many lives that were touched by him and left the better for it.

On the last day of my visit he taught me to drive a tractor, to milk a cow, and he gave me passing knowledge of the milk pasteurizing processes.

Returning to London I got on with my training, which was to last another six months. I was doing well and had rediscovered a facility for math. My social life was going along smashingly. I had moved into a small bed sitter in Hampstead that I shared with a new friend, Brian McNamara. We were to have some riotous times together.

Nineteen fifty-one was not a good year for me. I had exactly threepence by that cold February morning, Monday, a work day. The fare by tube to Cannon Street from Victoria, where my digs were, was sixpence so I started to walk, after eating a lettuce and bread sandwich and having a cup of tea.

I had worked it out that if I walked as far as Westminster, the threepence would take care of the fare from there on. I couldn't afford the embarrassment of being asked for excess fare, in view of the fact that I was dressed like a gentleman in bowler hat, umbrella, and with Friday's paper folded tightly so it looked like Monday's. Appearances, I had always been told, were paramount.

Walking in the gloomy half-light, I considered my predicament. Lack of cash and a dull job, eight until five pushing a pen. To my friends who didn't know, I was an assistant buyer for an engineering firm in the city. In actuality, I was a clerk pulling down four hundred pounds a year and trying to live and look as though I was in the thousand-a-year bracket.

Only one cheerful thought protruded. I had, through a polite club my aunt had strongly suggested I join, met a very nice Catholic girl who took her clothes off twice nightly in the Windmill Theatre. She was trying to get me into two folds, the Church's and her own. She also lent me money so that I could take her out.

Through Hazel, I had met, the previous Saturday, a lively group of drinkers in a pub in Hampstead, which in the next year was to become something of an institution among those who liked their mild and bitter, Woodbines and darts, mixed with conversation. Most English pubs, contrary to popular thought, are relatively dull.

One of these new acquaintances was George Price. He was to be my constant companion in my next few adventures. George was a character. He had been a Lieutenant Colonel of the Sudan Police Force, where he covered himself in glory in various suspect situations, until finally being asked to leave. During his last days in the country, he had married the seventeen-year-old daughter of a Sudan Railway official and was living in Hampstead in a one-room flat with her. George first commended himself by telling me in rapid succession three terribly funny stories about his experiences in the Sudan. Thus began my wildest dreams of working and living in Sudan...

George was impressive and I was impressionable. He was witty, attractive, a fine athlete and scholar, and possessed the type of mind that can remember obscure pieces of information. He had steel blue eyes, a square jaw, was cleft of chin, and had a piercing gaze. He had been expelled from Bedford school for starting a mutiny, which ruined his chances of becoming an officer in the Navy. George was probably the funniest man I had ever met.

With his help I had moved into a flat away from the detritus of Victoria Station and into the warm greyness of Hampstead. We had several commercial traveller-type pubs, an Odeon cinema, an underground train station, some larger shops, and a public swimming bath, which I had attended years prior, shivering and petrified, as a boy of twelve at my prep school.

I shared the flat, which was composed of one room, with a young man named Brian, who had lived in solid comfort with his Irish mother and stockbroker father in Surbiton, and had decided on a trial of the Bohemian life. He had the extraordinary ability of dropping his voice several octaves to achieve a chocolaty bass whenever an attractive girl was about. I tried for some months to emulate him without results. We had two beds arranged in an "L" shape so that the room was more like a drawing room with two couches.

The local pub I had been introduced to was the Duke of Hamilton. Not an attractive establishment, no historical associations, no interesting architecture, no added interests in the form of beer gardens or bowling alleys, it did not sell good beer and the host and his wife would not have won any popularity contests. What makes a popular pub is apparently indefinable. But the Duke was it, and it never occurred to anyone to go anywhere else.

I was very much taken with girls at this point, before which I'd had rather an odd life with women. I was very shy, frightened of embarrassment and of sex, which seemed fine in books and pictures, but rather uncomfortable in reality. I didn't get to grips with anything until I was twenty-six, which is innocent enough for anyone, God knows.

It was after one of our triumphs at the Duke that I met Georgina. She was the type of girl that the Scots would say was "fey." Even in Hampstead, which in nineteen fifty-three was Bohemian, she was a head turner. She wore skirts that were not really too long, but which she would wear so low on her hips, they practically brushed the ground. Her jerseys and blouses were always too small and she often looked like a child dressed in grown-up clothing. She had pale, cold eyes, widely-spaced and cat-like. I was captivated.

Georgina lived in with a wealthy family in Finchley. She looked after their children and our first date was to spend the evening baby-sitting together. The flat was on the second floor of what was in London a tall building at fifteen floors. It had a doorkeeper, a lift and was terribly smart. Shiny cars, mostly black, were in the parking lot, the shrubbery was well-kept, and inside, the lights were soft. I felt grand as I walked through the area and into the lobby, past the saluting guard and entered the elevator. I thought that it must be what America was like.

I rang the bell and one of the children opened the door. Upon meeting, Georgina and I had been violently passionate. But this night she was strangely distant. I decided to be cool and play it safe and so I concentrated on impressing the children with bad drawings on napkins, putting my cigarette in my mouth hot-end-first and anything else I could think of.

After the children had been put to bed and we were alone, Georgina changed moods and suggested we take a bath together. I brightly agreed, glad that, unusually for me, my socks were whole and my underwear new and clean. With pretended nonchalance. I undressed without looking at her as she removed her clothes.

We were together in the same steaming room. She was disappointingly thin, flat-breasted, and oddly square. For what I thought would be my first real experience, she was rather sexless. I got into the tub first and began soaping myself. She followed me, sat down and looked at me. A sad, distant look crossed her face. She remained immobile and gazed across the room into another time.

"You remind me of my brother," she said. He had been killed in the Battle of Britain I learned afterward.

"Would you please go now?" She exited the tub and stood towelling herself. Now of course I wanted her and said so.

"Please don't spoil things," she answered. She saw me to the door.

I took the elevator, crossed the lobby, the doorkeeper nodding and now uninteresting, out into a new, cold, spring night. The parking lot lights that had burned earlier warm and yellow were now frigidly blue. Steam escaped my mouth with each breath and the pavement rang distantly under my feet.

It always seemed that I was more successful with women when I was on the rebound. I was at a Sunday afternoon party on a gorgeous, sad, autumn day, the kind where you can hardly stand the beauty of it because you know it is the end of warmth and sunshine. As usual I was broke and had no cigarettes. We were drinking cider because it was cheap and fashionable for these Sunday gatherings. I badly wanted a cigarette but knew all the people in the flat so slightly that I could not ask them. I had been talking to a toothy girl who did not smoke and was desperately looking around for an escape, when the door was flung open and in walked an absolute vision.

Gwenda, her hair long and flowing, the colour of a new penny, and her colours altogether were what first attracted me to her. Her complexion was ivory, freckled. She had a full wide mouth and cheeks pink with the air, sparkling doe-like eyes and the brightest teeth I had ever seen – this, with a black velvety costume, which she wore with pearls at her throat. She advanced upon me with a flashing smile and looked directly at me. It was terribly unnerving. "Hello," she said.

"Hello, do you have a cigarette?"

She offered me a Players and a match. We went home by tube to Golders Green where she lived with a man and his family. I knew them and they knew me and had warned Gwenda against me. They might have been spot on; our relationship never did seem to go right.

My friends George and Berry, his wife, and I had stopped into the Duke one Saturday morning after groceries. It was quite empty and it smelled of stale beer and old cigarette smoke. The floor had just been waxed and fresh flowers were in bowls on the tables. A smoky coke fire had been lit and the beer seemed foamier than usual. We started to play a game of Skittles. George had, as usual, bought a shipping order of cigarettes, had taken one out, lit it, and placed it in his mouth. He took another one out and placed it in his Sudan silver case. The rest, still in the packet, he put into his pocket. This was in the event that someone asked him for one, at which point he would produce his case and with an elegant flick, open it. The asker would then say, "Oh sorry old boy, your last." It always worked and the practice had been adopted by many of our friends.

I met two heroes this day. Tony had been in the Royal Ulster Rifles. He served in the war and in Korea, where he had received a wound resulting in a steel plate in his head. He was a farm manager at the time and a discontented one at that. Tony was attractive to women but at first seemed innocuous in attitude and colouring. He lounged, but when he spoke, one listened.

Peter, the other hero, was quite the opposite. A talkative border Welshman with a stutter, the souvenir of surviving a burning Halifax bomber returning from

Germany. Peter Blandy, AFC and DFC, was just back from Mysore, India, where he had been planting tea. He was a dashing young man, well read, intelligent, and informative. His anecdotes about his experiences in India and elsewhere were the delight of the Saturday night crowd in the Duke. He would describe warm velvety nights there, cicadas shrilling outside, inside, fine china and silver and crystal, lights and music. It was so romantic. I felt like I had to experience it.

I believe the first seed was sown that night: I needed to get away. I didn't know where, but knew it had to be some place warm and exotic and exciting. Jungle, pampas, sullen tribesmen, and handsome swarthy women – that's what I wanted. These two hero Englishmen who had given a good deal to their country were uneasy in their country. They were restless and unsure of themselves here now. George, Berry, and I befriended them quickly.

Invitations were offered and accepted. We were to meet again at Tony's farm the following weekend. I was so excited at the prospect. The office routine seemed twice as dull and extended as usual. Friday and escape finally arrived.

I left the office on Cannon Street that night, walking out with the crowd, but felt different and separate. I walked as though I was already on the way to nameless forests, deep and unexplored, and I was, in a sense, even if it was only beginning in a Buckinghamshire farmhouse. I fell asleep on the train.

I woke to hear porters announcing incoherent station names as the train jerked and bumped to a crawl, and then, with a final gasp, stopped. I looked out of the window and saw that it was the stop before mine. Arriving ten or so minutes later, I got out and walked across the bridge to the station yard, gave up my ticket and walked through the gate to see a Land Rover parked in front.

"I imagine you need a drink," said Tony. He, Peter, George, and Berry were all there. Berry grabbed my arm and said that as guests we were to sit in the front. Tony was driving and George and Peter sat in the back. We roared out of the station yard but came to a precipitate halt.

"Well here we are. If we're going to do a pub crawl, let's start at the first pub!"

I'm sure we talked about it during the night and made plans, but when I was woken at what seemed to be the middle of the night because the fox wouldn't wait for us, I really had no idea what anyone was talking about. A crashing hangover didn't help.

"What fox?" I asked, gulping scalding coffee.

"The hunt man, the fox hunt. We're following in the Land Rover."

"Good God Payne you have a shocking memory!"

After breakfast I felt more human. We set out in the Land Rover, all five of us suitably provisioned with sandwiches, which Berry had made. George thoughtfully provided several crates of brown ale and Peter a flask of whiskey to keep the cold out for it was still early April.

We drove up and down and round and round the narrow, enormously hedged Buckinghamshire lanes. Peter was determined to keep the nose of the car pointed down the centre. George chortled and gurgled in the back with an occasional rude word bandied at people on foot.

We arrived at the meet in time to see the hind end of some horses, stragglers, gate-openers, and those who wanted one more suck at the Stirrup Cup. Peter crashed into second gear and we whined up the hill after the main body.

A beautiful young woman with china blue eyes and porcelain skin, bowler-hatted, veiled, and riding side-saddle pointed across some beet fields. Peter geared down and put the Rover into four-wheel drive, spun the steering wheel around and headed through the open gate and across country. In the distance, as we lurched up and down through the rough folds of ground, I caught a glimpse of scarlet moving rapidly.

"Christ!" said Tony, "I believe we're in amongst the leaders."

We had unwittingly short-cutted and had only the master, a half dozen or so riders, and the dogs between us and the fox.

"Tally Ho!" cried George, interrupting his concentration on a bottle of Watney's Best Brown Ale.

We bumped and rolled into and across a hollow heavily shrubbed and treed, through a small wood, and found ourselves in the middle of a council of war amongst the leading hunters.

I was about to say, "well, what do we do now?" when the low gear was slipped in and off we lurched down the meadow, careening between sedge and willow, until, with one drunken swoop, we slid sideways into water.

I was alarmed by this point. I could swim, but the

water would have been so cold. The others had a wild, glazed look in their eyes. I decided I must be in the company of criminal lunatics and my life would end in the icy grip of this obscure midland river. Then, good old Rover gave out a crashing fart, engaged all its gears, stripped them, re-engaged them, and surged forward, even though up to its axles in water, muck, and slime.

We passed a startled-looking hound as he was swimming. He looked over at us and trod water as we ground by. With one last despairing plunge we rose out of the water. We stood on the farther bank shaking water off while stock was taken. I believe the experience of crossing the creek had had a salutary influence on our driver and navigator, for there was definite pause in the festivities.

The hounds and horses had fled across a arising feature to our front and disappeared across the watery skyline.

The day had developed into that typical English horror: starting out blue, but soon dropping water like a bad cold. I was chilled, and horrified when, at the end of the chase, they had grounded the fox to home. This was the part I had dreaded, and wondered about. The chase had been exciting and fun but the killing chilled my blood. It was over quickly. I had my eyes still shut, listening to the sustained laughter, heavy breathing, and the much clumsy motion amidst the smells of sweat and hot blood.

"Here is the brush. By God you deserve it."
I opened my eyes to see the china face and doll-like eyes, the transparent veil and flushed features, with arm extended. In her hand, a furry tail. It was flung into the

Rover, and trying to put on a brave face, I picked it up and looked at George. He looked away and said to Peter in a sober voice, "Let's find the nearest pub." We drove to the closest village in silence.

It was nineteen fifty-four. Tony had gotten married, Peter was still about, though we didn't see him much. I was living with George and Berry in the mews flat. George was working for a group of private policemen and property guardians. Gwenda and I were friends again, Berry was getting plumper and plumper, and England was on the way to winning the Test Match for the first time in years. It promised to be a good year.

I had just gone to a job interview to be a salesman for wallpaper with headquarters in a noisome part of Camden Town. The factory backed onto another factory that made cigarettes with cork tips, and which sported a gigantic plaster black cat on top of a concrete edifice that was also false-fronted and glassed.

"Why don't you apply for this job?" George asked on a Sunday over tea. "Executive Engineer. Group of Sudan companies require young, gregarious man experienced in diesel engine practise, theoretical and practical irrigation, and sales and general engineering." George read the insertion from the Telegraph.

"First of all, I'm not an engineer. I did two years of

engineering school at night and dropped out. I have never sold anything, and they are bound to want someone who can speak Arabic fluently."

George, who had already spent many years in the Sudan, was interested on my behalf. I believe he saw in helping me a certain follow-through of his own prematurely interrupted time in the country. He helped me to write an absolutely marvellous letter of application. It got me an interview.

The answering letter was couched in terms of the most beautiful Victorian colonial office redundancy, and yet oddly, went straight to the point. I was charmed, though indeed, pessimistic.

The meeting was set for a Friday afternoon in May. It was the sort of day that starts the thoughts rising toward places beyond the seas. It never seems to matter how many times one travels abroad to distant warmer climates, to various palm-rimmed shores. The desire for a change, even to places one knows are less than happy, was strong.

I started out to my interview with trepidation. I had arranged for the meeting to take place at a time that would not embarrass my present position: during the latter part of my lunch hour.

The offices of Sudan Mercantile London were in that area of London that never seems to alter, come Hitler's bombs and changes in Borough Council. Though the trams are no longer underground at the northern part of Holborn, the angled tracks leading down to the gated darkness still exist. The theatres of the Aldwych still advertise those moth-eaten plays that seem to go on from the time they were introduced long ago in some hopeless middle England town, to never-ending success, hosting Wednesday matinees and evenings for the old ladies of Kensington and their nephews.

I handed in the ticket at the gate and climbed the escalator to the street. Normally at this time of day this station and area would have been quite deserted. So, I was surprised to find a crowded entrance at street level. Music of a martial nature sounded, clashing drums and cymbals, horses clopping and that awakening sound of a crowd that senses something approaching.

Hats were removed. I saw a policeman of the city of London – taller, wearing an odd helmet and without a tie, with blue and white armlets on his cuff-salute.

"What's going on?" I asked a flustered woman with a black shiny hat.

"The Queen is visiting the city."

I could see the procession, the centre part of it stretched a city block or two. God knew how long the rear escort went. I had just five minutes to be on time.

How to get across that road? I wanted the job, I knew I wanted it badly. I needed it. I wriggled through the crowd, pushed aside two be-wigged barristers, presumably on their lunch break, and worked my way past a perspiring guardsman standing rigidly to a royal salute.

Nothing between me and the other side of the road but a copper, some mounted police and a couple of St. John's Ambulance men. I took life, honour, and future into my hands and ran.

I arrived at the offices on Holborn somewhat

dishevelled. Hurriedly dusting myself down, a quick wipe of the shoe for shine with my handkerchief, the tie straightened, and I was inside the cool marble-floored foyer. It was dark and difficult to see at first, and to get my bearings. On one side was an old-fashioned Victorian personal elevator, and on the other, a register of tenants behind a glass front. Peering through the gloom, I ascertained that Keymer, Son & Co., and Sudan Mercantile Co. had offices in London, Khartoum, Port Sudan, and, oh joy, Wad Medani! What pictures were conjured. Hot, white stuccoed houses, verdant green getting greener by Nile-side but more yellow as it encroached onto the desert and until it was digested into the wilderness.

I was already some ten minutes late. The lift creaked and groaned to the fourth floor with some alarming pauses and jerks on the way up. The gates opened and crashed to one side. The whole floor smelled musty and decadent, like a long-forgotten book opened after years of neglect.

I knocked on the door marked in gold with the company name and walked in. It was like a room out of Kipling. The only thing missing: a ceiling fan. The space inside was a fairly large room divided by wood and glass partitions. In the nearest one to me was an ancient leather-faced gentleman who looked up at me from a littered desk over pince-nez. I explained who I was and he consulted a vertigrised half-hunter attached by a fine gold chain to some connection lost in layers of shifting sweaters and cardigans.

"You're eleven and a half minutes late."

I began to explain, but the glare he gave me decided my silence.

"Wait here."

He returned after a minute or two and motioned me through a door to the right and at the back of the hall. "Mr. Keymer will see you now."

I went through the doorway not knowing exactly what to expect. A young-looking man in his middle forties, with clear eyes and a well-tanned face, rose immediately from behind an enormous desk and walked with long purposeful strides around to shake my hand. "I'm Kenneth Keymer."

After some years in India and East Africa and after his father's death, Kenneth Keymer had taken over the running of the London office. Ronald, his brother, ran the Khartoum end. Kenneth was jovial, boisterous, and thoroughly charming. He put me at ease immediately, no talk of minutes late. He got right to the point of what the job would entail, the details of the contract, the history and present position of the company, the salary (twice as much as I was then earning) and the date of departure were I to be hired.

"Now, why do you wish to go to the Sudan?"

I had no real, coherent reason. I gathered my thoughts. It all came out in an unco-ordinated flood, all the pent-up dreams and rasping frustrations of the post-war years, the passionate desire to get to a country that would allow me to breathe, and to a job that would straighten my ambitions. I told him about the emotional attachments I had with the country, even mentioning that I had seen the movie "The Four Feathers" seven times. I had read all I could about that section of Africa and could reel off the names of several tribes, their locations, their principal occupations and day-to-day activities. I stopped, suddenly embarrassed, to find him looking at me strangely. "How well do you get on with people?" he asked.

"Well, I served for four years on the lower deck of the Royal Navy and never got into a serious fight."

"Well, that's something." He rubbed his chin. "My brother will be coming out next month and will want to meet you. Leave your office and home telephone numbers in case we need to get in touch with you." With a last friendly smile and a handshake, he indicated an end to the interview.

The parade was over outside and I walked back to the tube station and returned to the office one hour late for the afternoon's work, to receive ice-cold looks and reminders of my duties, which included punctuality, but somehow I didn't care.

I had moved away from George and Berry and had set up housekeeping with a brother and sister and the brother's girlfriend. It was a very pleasant existence. I had a little room in which it was impossible to stand upright. It was so small that the doorknob got into bed with you when the door was opened. We shared a kitchen and a living room and split the rent four ways.

Roger and his sister Margaret were in the theatre. Roger's girlfriend, Felicity, worked in a large London hospital as a dietician. She would only eat carrots (and these only ground to a pulp), nuts, green vegetables, and a peculiar toadstool tea. Other than her eating habits, she was an attractive person given to walking around in her underwear. Margaret and Felicity looked after my small wants, cooking for us men, sewing and mending when necessary.

The flat was in an older part of Hampstead – Fitzjohn's Avenue – halfway up to the Whitestone Pond, the Spaniard's Pub, and the highest of three hills overlooking London.

Though the workdays were dull, the evenings and weekends were full of fun, good conversation, wine, beer, and music. We all loved the same composers and I was introduced to many that I pretended to know.

Weeks had elapsed since my interview with Keymer. It was now early summer and I had given up hope of hearing from them again. I had been too eager I decided, or too ill-informed. Whatever the reasons, another crossroads had been passed and I was determined to buckle down and work harder at my art school studies in the evenings.

I had been going to Saint Martins in the Tottenham Court Road now for some two years. I studied advertising, design layout, general drawing, and fabric design. This also included the rudimentaries of interior decorating and design. I was something of a character at the school as I was older than most of the students. Coming straight from the city, wearing my bowler hat, dark suit, and black shoes gave my erstwhile companions some room for comparison as the uniform in those days typically consisted of blue jeans, sweaters, long hair and sandals.

I had a very fine scholarly Australian instructor who told me early in the term to forget drawing, as my talent was barely a facility, and that there were many more competent students half my age who might go twice as far. In spite of, or perhaps because of, this advice we became good friends and drinking companions. We would go to all the little basement clubs of Soho, which cost half a crown to join for perpetuity, and where the doorkeepers were typically bearded and sandaled, with an unbuttoned, green and gold uniform jacket. We were surrounded with cheap beer, sausage and eggs, chess, smoky walls, and long-haired girls and boys. We spent most of our evenings in such haunts that last year at home.

I was designing and constructing a float for the Chelsea Arts Ball, which was held annually in the Albert Hall in early January. Each art school in London competed to produce the most bizarre, original, and exotic float. Our effort was to do the South Seas and we had the best looking and largest busted models we could muster. They were to wear fish tails and long, flaxen wigs, which would be stuck to their breasts with adhesive. The float was to be erected that night without me.

I returned home to an empty flat and found a note to call a Mr. Keymer as soon as possible the next morning. I slept very badly that night and was up at what George used to call a "sparrow's fart." I knew somehow that I had got the job. I couldn't quite understand why, but a gnawing feeling told me this was not just another interview. I fiddled around making tea and waiting for the time that I could wake up the others to have someone to talk to.

I finally couldn't stand it any longer and went into Margaret's bedroom. She was fast asleep and the room was dark. I could hear her breathing softly through her mouth, a slight snore, sibilant and rustling gently. I went over and stood, looking down. This kind, good-hearted girl would give her last cigarette away and lend me bus fare, not minding when I forgot to repay.

It was eight-thirty when I called the Keymer office.

"Oh yes, Payne," said Mr. Keymer, "I'm glad you called." He seemed so nonchalant, too casual. "My brother was delayed but he would like to meet you. Can you make it at one-thirty today?"

I replied that I could and would, now suddenly disappointed by the tone of his voice, and yet so elated that they had not entirely given me up.

Ronald Keymer was everything his brother was not. Where Kenneth was open and cordial, Ronald was cold and acerbic. He had an odd habit of looking at people directly, but constantly blinking due to some nervous tic. Physical motion without the spiritual connection, yet one knew that a fine brain was behind that fine head, that this was not a robot, but a keen incisive mind.

I again went through my reasons for wanting the job, and explained what I felt I could offer the company and the country. Through it all, Kenneth looked nervously at his brother and then out the window. Ronald sat looking at me with his red-rimmed eyes and his watery moustache, which he plucked intermittently in absolute silence. I stammered through my explanations and glanced appealingly at Kenneth.

Ronald yawned, and as though signalled, Kenneth looked up. "Thank you Payne. That will be all. Well Ronald, I imagine you're tired."

With feverish movements, Kenneth hovered over Ronald as if to protect him from any sordid contact with the outside world. "Yes, I think I had better see Mother. Well Payne, we have an imponderable or two to discuss. Good of you to come and see us and though we are most encouraged at our meetings with you, we would like to be frank enough to say that if you have any other offers outstanding, please do not turn them down because of our conversation. We will advise you of our decision. Goodbye."

I was absolutely deflated. It was two-thirty in the afternoon and as I had given some excuse to my office manager that I would not be in again that day, and as it was a Friday, I decided to stop at the nearest pub and start alone a night that would never be forgotten entirely.

I began at a pub I would not normally have chosen to drink in, only that it was nearby did it attract me. I wanted to start quickly so that all these serious things in my mind, all these worries and trepidations, would retreat into a comfortable alcoholic haze. I had several at the Cock, a pub on the Holborn, and then walked down to the Strand.

I found, after an hour or two, that it was not drink that I needed, but companionship. Someone to tell all to. I knew no one in this part of London, so got out into the street and went towards the nearest bus stop to head home.

The cool air hit me immediately and made me dizzily tight.

I found a bus stop and climbed aboard an already moving number thirteen. Although I could not read the number without my glasses, instinctively I knew it was the bus that went to Cannon Street by way of Charing Cross and Fleet Street, St. Paul's, and down the Strand, up past Trafalgar and the statues and the Tate, along Leicester Square and the theatres and cinemas and taxi ranks to Coventry Street, that connects the serious theatre with the brashness of Wrigley chewing gum, neon lights, Eros and the Circus, up the sweep of Regents, past Swan and Edgar's, to Oxford Street and the crossroads of Commerce. A sharp left and Selfridges loomed in the distance on the right like a mammoth's shadow in early evening mists. Right angle away from the lights, the smell of money and chocolate, and past the last hanging tree of London and the marble arch, which holds the smallest police station in town.

Suddenly, the quiet of the streets behind the highways, the meandering beginning of Baker Street that led past Daniel Neal where my clothes were bought from nursery to prep school, all the way up to Madame Tussaud's and the fish and chips shops of Welbeck, the surgeries of fashion in the Harley Street complex, the flannelled fools in the spring and summer on the left, where one can't quite see over the high fences of Lord's cricket ground when a hit is made, past the purlieus of St. John's Wood and Marylebone to Swiss Cottage and the north.

As though it never happened, the bus journey that I had made twice a day for three years, which had become so tedious and tiresome, became like a cinema flickering past, seen through a watery screen of pale violets and blues and greys, sad and bygone before they are realised, like happy moments on dreary days.

I got off the bus in my evening of drunken forgetfulness – it was now too late for the pubs – they had closed in the half hour or so that I had been dreaming. It was just as well as I was overwrought, tired, and now that the bitter beer and bittersweet visions and thoughts had worked off into the cold night, it was bed that I needed.

The following Monday, as I surveyed my desk and the back of my manager's head, I was filled with the direst forebodings. Even the thought of an interesting evening at Saint Martins failed to rouse me from my depression. I got through it somehow and got on the same bus that had been the vessel for my voyage of discovery.

At art class that night I played with my pencils, taking no real notice of my instructor and at the first break I left by the side door, got into the now hateful number thirteen bus and went home, half-formed thoughts in my mind. Did I remember someone saying that you had to be a member of the Seaman's Union before you could go to sea as a merchant sailor? I had to get away, somehow, somewhere.

I walked into the flat and there was Margaret as before with a piece of paper in her hand.

"It's them again," she said.

I snatched the paper from her hand. It read: "IT IS IMPORTANT THAT YOU CALL KENNETH KEYMER AS EARLY AS POSSIBLE TOMORROW MORNING.

The Duke of Hamilton Pub

The Duke of Hamilton Pub

fading skyline finely drawn

mist driven light descending

dark formed green mystery seen

formless forests ending...

"Can you leave for Khartoum the twenty-second?" That was two weeks away.

"Yes Sir." I was astounded.

"Right. We will post you all the confirmatory details which you will receive tomorrow morning, but briefly so that you know what is to be done, here are the bare essentials. You have a current passport?"

"Yes."

"You must obtain visas for permanent residence in the Anglo-Egyptian Sudan and a transit visa for Egypt. They are very sticky about things like that, particularly if you're British and have to stay longer than a day or so. Go to your doctor and have him certify that you are fit for service in the tropics, then have your shots for yellow fever, malaria, dysentery, typhoid, et cetera. Tell the doctor where you're going and have a shot for everything. By the way, do you drink?"

A startling question at this stage of the game.

"Well, not much," I said, "but I will if you want me to."

"Capital. If you don't, you'll be under rather unusual stress. Right. What's next? A note has just come through on the question of a tropical kit allowance. Mr. Keymer in Khartoum advises that a new policy dictates that fifty pounds Egyptian will be allotted to all new staff, beginning with you, for clothing requirements. Alright Payne, I'd like you to fill out all the necessary contracts we shall send you and mail them back to me immediately. I will call you when I get them back along with your clearance papers from the Sudan Government Agency. Perhaps we can lunch together then."

I kissed everyone in sight, Margaret, Felicity, on her way to the hospital. I would have rushed out and embraced everyone on the street. It is an odd thing that it always seems to be sunny when good news is about. When happy things occur, the skies always seem to be blue and gold. I went to work in the city that day, one and a half hours late. I still felt guilty. How conditioned I had become.

Handing in my notice was not as bad as I had expected. The president, who looked like a petulant bulldog, hardly even looked up and growled, "Africa, eh? Well, kill a couple of Mau-Mau for me." I started to explain that the Khartoum was several hundred miles north from Kenya, but decided not to when faced with the patently uninterested expanse of gleaming pink scalp that was turned towards me.

I had a week and a few days to get all the shots needed, arrange for the various papers and documents necessary for entry and transit, and to purchase some suitable clothes. I stood in line the following day at the Hospital for Tropical Diseases in the Euston Road, and looking ahead, was watching the nurse plunging a needle into the arms of a young couple and their four children, who, from the conversation, were on their way to West Africa. After the last tiny arm was swabbed and stabbed, it was my turn.

After wiping and squeezing, the doctor held the needle poised, and for a second or two looked keenly into my eyes and said, "No alcohol for twenty-four hours." The shock of the statement was worse than the prick as the needle went in.

We all met at the Duke that evening. It was to be one of the last times I was to be together with all my friends. I drank ginger ale.

The following night, Saturday, an enormous party was thrown. There must have been two hundred people, some of whom I didn't even know. Complete strangers were kissing and hugging me and telling me how much they would miss me. It was rather fun and rather sad. Some time around six I was helped out to a cab and driven home.

Sunday was a repeat. I don't know what time I went finally to sleep Sunday night, but I awoke Monday morning to the loud honking of a car horn outside and then the bell ringing stridently. I sat up in horror not knowing the time. All I needed was to have overslept and missed the plane. I rushed to the door more dead than alive, a headache and nausea ensuing. I opened the door. There stood a chum who drove a taxi.

"You'd better get cracking," he said. "We've got an hour to get to Victoria Air Terminal."

Thank God we made it. I blessed this thoughtful man who was rushing around packing my last few possessions while I shaved and drank pints of tomato juice while he was standing impatiently at the door. I crept into Margaret's room for the last time and kissed her goodbye as she slept. I climbed into the car and I was off at last on the way to adventures and unimaginable dangers. This was the first leg. I couldn't breathe I was so excited.

We got to the air terminal and I thanked Bill and

started to pay for the fare. "No," he grunted and looked away roughly, "it's on the house. Good luck."

A brisk, cool, and attractive young woman looked over my papers for ticketing. "Yes, you're going on a Sudan Government Plane." She stamped a couple of sheets, clipped something to something and handed back my packet. "You join that group over there," she explained, motioning to a small cluster of people in a corner. "A bus will take you to Heathrow. You've time for a cup of tea, the restaurant is open."

I thanked her and went over to join the others. We were eventually collected by another cool young thing who shepherded us to a small bus waiting outside. There were about ten of us, two of whom were women with spectacles and severe hairstyles. They told me they were Methodist Missionaries headed for a particularly troubled part of Central Africa: the Southern Equatorial Province of the Sudan, which was to experience considerable bloody turmoil some years later.

We drove through the quiet streets of Southwest London. It was still very early and there was a heavy white summer fog lying thickly around. I was disappointed as this would be the last I would see of London for some time and I wanted to imprint the picture on my mind. I sat back and gazed out of the window thinking of all the people I would never see again and of this great city that I might not see again either. The terribly lonely, enormously sad feeling that I was always to have thereafter when leaving a place I have stayed in for a long time, crept over me. The initial excitement gave way to an anti-climactic lump in my throat.

The enormity of what I was doing and what I had

done enveloped me. Could I handle the job? Worse, could I stand the kind of life I imagined it would be? Forebodings of the worst kind and nightmarish considerations preceded panic. Was it too late? I could stop the bus, get out, and run, anywhere.

The bus slowed and turned in through some gates, went up a long drive and through some trees, and then stopped in front of a large Nissen hut. It was too late.

I pulled myself together and stood up. We all got off the bus and trooped through the now-clearing mist to the doorway. Inside it was quite insufferably hot and the room was crowded with people and noises. I thrust my way through the crowd and found a seat between two children who were playing cowboys and Indians. Sitting back and lighting a cigarette I examined my fellow passengers. In almost all cases, they were nondescript. Teachers, nurses, or government officials of one sort or another. I had become quite blasé already and had not yet even set foot in Africa.

A voice on the Tannoy loudspeaker system advised us to pick up our belongings and move to the gateway. We were checked through and I found myself walking across the hard tarmac towards the aircraft. This was the first time I had ever flown and I was filled with frantic curiosity. The airplane was a Vicker's Viking, a two-engined, low-winged monoplane. The body looked suspiciously thinly covered, as though it were a frame and fabric-skinned machine from the First World War. It might have been for all I knew.

Being a Sudan Government aircraft charter, there were no hostesses or other similar comforts. One steward met us sourly as we boarded and there was a generally amateurish air about the whole crew, as though they were bored and hung over. Otherwise, all the other passengers seemed calm and orderly.

I relaxed as much as I could, swallowed thickly and climbed the short flight of steps to the cabin door. Having an old-fashioned undercarriage, the airplane sat in an inclined position like a squatting gull, so I had to climb up a fairly steeply tilted passageway towards the front, where my seat was. This made the experience more alarming for me. I was the only seat facing backwards, about which I was not happy. There was nothing but the crew and their controls between me and the nose that was about to cut through infinity at some six hundred miles per hour.

I settled into the seat and found it to be surprisingly comfortable. I was facing a stern woman wearing blue eyeglasses. She was sucking on a sweet and had white cotton wool sprouting from each ear. She eyed me oddly and for so long a time that I was forced to look away.

With an ear shattering, coughing, sputtering series of explosions the starboard engine was fired up, belched clouds of oily black and grey smoke, and then stopped. The whole airplane shuddered.

"Would you like a boiled sweet and some wool for the altitude change?" the blue eyeglasses fixed me with a glare. I accepted the sweet and declined the wool. I wanted to hear what was happening in the frightening aircraft. I remembered my father's tales of his early flights in an SE5A and of being sent back to the trenches in the machine gun cavalry because he was too tall to fit in the cockpit. My father had been the tallest man in the Royal Scot's Fusiliers.

The pilot had evidently fiddled around with something as this time we started with a much healthier roar. First the starboard engine fired and almost at once the other. They ran roughly for a few minutes and then the smoke cleared and they settled into a sweet, resonant purr. The plane moved forward in a series of jerks, pointing first this way then that, and then we rolled out slowly to the end of the runway The noise level rose to an unbearable scream as the pilot revved up as a final test.

I gripped the seat with white-knuckled apprehension, when, with a marvellously relieving feeling, I knew I could not control my destiny any longer. Maximum thrill with minimum danger. We were off and running at an extraordinary speed. In less than seconds, the tail wheel was off the ground and I was now level, which made me feel much better. I looked out the window and saw the ground rushing past in the distance, the green and olive fields and hedgerows. It was exactly what I had imagined.

With a bang, the undercarriage was slammed back into the belly and the plane banked sharply to the right. We cleared the airport buildings, the plane straightened out, and began a steady roaring climb. I sat with my eyes glued to the window. The thick white, blue, and grey clouds floated by like fat cushions of cream about to burst. I felt a tapping at my knee. I looked up. It was the blue eye-glassed teacher opposite me. "Where are you going?" she asked.

When I told her, she nodded and told me that the city of Khartoum was a hotbed of all that is corrupt in the Sudan. "Arab spiced with the worst of Europe and brutalised by the sullen blacks."

I distractedly tried to listen and at the same time my mind wandered to the future. A slant of sun flashed across her face and made her squint. I looked out and saw this fantastic cloud castle built up on top of other castles. Down in the depths were blued valleys, full of mystery and shadow.

We were at about seven thousand feet and the clouds were falling fast below the airplane. The sky was an incomprehensible blue. I was over any apprehension I had felt and wondered how anyone could be afraid of flying. I needed two things, a pee and a drink. I unstrapped the seatbelt and, feeling as though everyone in the plane were watching me, started gingerly back to the tail.

"Can I help you Sir?" asked the steward.

"Yes. Would you send a double scotch and soda to my seat please? And, is the lavatory occupied?"

"Yes, and no, Sir." He smiled and made me feel quite grand.

I went into the tiny compartment and shut the door. Standing there felt very strange. I smiled as I thought to myself of all the childish thoughts about peeing we were surrounded with growing up. About going to the lavatory in general and how delicate it was, how people shouldn't see and making sure your bottom was wiped clean. Here I was at seven or eight thousand feet wetting on the south coast of England. Absolutely gorgeous.

My fellow passenger was holding my drink in a little paper napkin when I got back to my seat. "Here's your scotch."

"Thank you. May I get you one?"

"No, I don't drink, thank you."

I was not accustomed to scotch but this seemed a good one. I let the aroma breathe up into my nostrils as I took a long swallow. It burst somewhere between my throat and the top part of my chest first, then after almost choking, but not quite, the warmth seeped gently into my arms and lower abdomen, then into my legs. As I started to take a puff on a newly lit cigarette, the lingering warmth from my drink caressed the area behind my eyes and subsided into a great glowing ball in suspension between the top of my head and the tips of my toes.

I was completely relaxed and was sipping idly on my second when we were to start the descent. The first landfall was about to appear. We had been flying now for what seemed to be only a matter of an hour or so, but what was in reality some four or more. We had crossed the channel and flown southeasterly, crossing the French coast near Marseilles. We were now turning steeply to land at the Nice airport.

Twisting around as we dropped lower and lower I could see the water below turn in colour. The deep areas were an eerie, unpleasant bluish black, more shallow areas were a friendlier aquamarine, and then the shallow areas were a brilliant turquoise, flashing and iridescent. The water was so thin and the sun so strong that I could see the sand, white and silver on the bottom of the sea. I felt as though I was suspended over a precious jewel made more rare than others because it was in constant movement, though set in a world of stillness.

The runway appeared, a dazzling white concrete and gravel expanse built out on the edge of the sea. In the distance were lemon yellow fields, trees with gnarled trunks and branches, and flashes of blue sparked with white – inlets of the Mediterranean coursing into the tummy of France. The Maritime Alps were visible, sloping majestically in a series of giant steps, first beige, and then rosy tan, pale blue-green, mauve-violet, and grey tipped with creamy white. They remained a mysterious, uncaring, rigid barrier between unequivocal north and warm and fervent south.

My bones whitened again as I braced myself for the connection between man in machine and ground. With a very bad bump, we collided, wheels screaming, protesting, and bouncing. One moment further in purgatory. A second bump, not so bizarre as the first, and the wheels attached themselves to the ground. We struck and rolled along the strip, attached as though it would be impossible for us to ever get off the ground again.

The tail wheel bumped gratefully down and almost in an imitation of the moves prior to take off, a hundred years ago in another world, the plane jerked at angles of forty-five degrees from our leading front. Jerk, jerk, bump, point, until we resumed a slow forward motion, nose upward. Breast and wings were spread and pouty like a proud pigeon returning to its benevolent master.

We stopped in front of some huts bleached white and sandy in the midday sunshine. The engines cut off abruptly. From then on, until the following morning, I was almost deaf. All I could discern were lips mouthing at me, no sounds at all coming from them. My nose and ears were stopped up completely, my head ached and I was hung over from the two double scotches. The doors opened and we filed out onto a low platform attached to a small stepladder.

The first feeling of being on earth again after one's first flight must rank with all the great firsts in a life: that first bicycle ride when you know your father's hands are not on the back of the saddle, or the first time you discover you will not drown after the bigger boy has thrown you into the deep end.

Lunch was served inside one of the buildings, which was comparatively cool after the oppressive heat outside. A delicious onion soup, some whitebait followed by veal with green salad, vanilla ice cream and fruit, with the wine of the province – bitter but refreshing. We smoked our cigarettes and gazed out of the window at the airplane as it was being serviced.

After lunch, service, and re-fuelling, we rolled once more down the runway. I was oddly a little more nervous the second time. Did one become more careful as one mastered the bicycle? Was one more nervous the second time they rode a horse, drove a car, or flew in an airplane?

We cleared the ground and climbed away to the left, engines struggling for breath, higher and higher, the air carrying us as the water does the fish, finding levels of solidity to ride on until another push up of stronger air is found to coincide with the pull of the two steel propellers. They tug and sigh as they endeavour to extract from the air in front of them enough suction to keep the body moving through the vacuum in front.

We were at eight thousand feet in no time and flying over the sea heading towards the island of Malta, which was to be our stop for the night. The little gallant airplane buzzed through the mid-afternoon sun on the lovely, slightly misty, blue day. The sea, so far below, shone and glinted as a thousand million sunbeams bounced off its surface, with tiny specks weaving, rippling white and gold threads between them.

Freighters or liners ploughed through the waves, and I remembered those days when the convoy work I did in my little ship made similar marks, so temporary across the face of the changing ocean. It had then seemed so permanent, the plumes of disturbed water as the bombs blew and the depth charges exploded. Here, I was now in the reversed position. So this is how the little ships looked to the Stuka and the Regia Aronautica, to the Capronis and the Dormers. It was so easy from up here, the tiny sea craft below so helpless and slow, staggering across the painted blue, obvious and clumsy in their movements.

It started to get dark and the sky began to glimmer as the sun started to hiss into the sea. Lights started to come on below. I must have dropped off again for I was shaken by my companion in blue glasses, again with the admonition that seat belts were to be fastened during our descent into Valetta in Malta. I was curious about this island that had been heavily attacked by both the Italians and the Germans in the last war; so badly damaged and so bravely defended that His Majesty George VI had seen fit to award en masse the decoration of the George Cross to the entire population, both military and civilian.

This was my first view of a city at night from the air. The central downtown hub was brightly lit, and sparkled like a bunch of vari-coloured fireworks in the hands of a badly controlled child. Reds, blues, greens, fluorescent flashes as trams brushed their wires, traffic lights, neon signs all competing with one another for gaudiness.

The Viking swooped down to its last level prior to the actual landing pattern. We extinguished cigarettes. The engines throttled back, and with a bump, the wheels groaned down, clicked, and locked. We glided, gently to the terminal. This part of flight has always fascinated me the most: the return of the bird to Earth, the skill of the pilot in controlling this enormous craft, heavy with oily steaming engines, struts, flooring, intricate controls, light steel skin and rubber wheels and baggage all in the hands of two men. But this was to be a bad landing. We hit the ground much too fast, rebounded into the air rising and falling to thump down again, with rubber protesting as it struck the ground.

The plane ran along the concrete at level position then as it slowed, the body started to sag like a tired old gentleman. Then the tail wheel grounded and we were at the normal three-wheeled position rolling along slower and slower, engines droning as though they were being run inside out. We stopped at the end of the strip, turned around, and slowly taxied back to the terminal buildings.

We exited the airplane into the warmth of the summer evening. It was dusk in the central Mediterranean. I had been to Valletta as a child on the way back from Port Said when Daddy worked for the Shell Company and for the Iraq Petroleum Company, but I was so young then that nothing intelligent came back as a reminder.

We were met by a limousine and a small bus. I was fortunate enough to get into a large and comfortable Humber of immediately post-war vintage. It had the same large desert-type balloon tires that my father's staff car had when he was Embarkation Staff Officer in Stranraer.

My companions were the SDF Officers along with a couple of others in the Police Force. I was determined to tell them about my friendship with George and perhaps hear old stories of exploits long ago. We all got on very well and when we got to the hotel were already making plans to meet at the bar and have dinner together. The hotel was one of the finest and most luxurious in the area and as it was a new hotel, built since the war, one of the finest in Eastern Europe. Enormous, graceful, and white, the Phoenicia stood protectively above the rest of downtown Valletta, new, bright and clean, born of rubble, dirt, dust, and blood.

Glasses tinkled and music played softly. Our feet sank in thick resilient carpet. Evening-suited waiters and starched bellhops moved about busily, elegant, and smart. I felt shabby and dirty and was glad to get away into my bathroom, which was almost as big as the suite itself and had thick towels warming on hot rails. My sheets were turned back and a note reminding me to leave my shoes in the corridor for shining had been left on a table.

I took a lukewarm bath and lay back and relaxed for a few minutes before getting dressed and heading down to the bar. The bar was reasonably full, although no one that I was to meet had come down yet. I ordered a scotch with soda and ice, lit a Players, took a long drink, put the glass down and surveyed the room.

The crowd at the bar was a polyglot of a few Maltese and a number of English and Americans, Scandinavians, Germans, and a sprinkling of Levantines, Greeks, and Italians. It was all very scrumptious and sophisticated. I really felt like a man of the world. A dark swarthy waiter approached me.

"Mr. Payne? Kaimakan Fitzgerald and his friends ask if you would join them in the men's bar."

"Ah, thank you." I was quite flattered that the waiter should unerringly pick me out, and tipped him rather more handsomely than was proper. I finished my drink, stubbed out a cigarette and left the room following the waiter.

We went up a short staircase, past some large French windows that looked out onto the harbour, all lit up like a Christmas tree, down along carpeted corridor and out to the terrace with the fountains.

It was so quiet. Except for the soft music that filtered from some dance room somewhere in the hotel, there were no other sounds to interrupt the beauty of the evening. When the doors were opened with a flourish into the man's bar, I was not prepared for the crash of sound that came out, hitting me almost like a solid wall.

The place was jammed. There was shouting and singing, laughter and argument, a hot raucous crowd, some in uniform, but most in civvies. I looked around a little afraid. I could see no friendly face amongst these beefy, red, shining, and waving heads. It was like an enormous public cocktail party for men only, not my cup of tea at all. I was about to turn around and leave when my name was called out.

"Ted! Over here! Come and have a drink, there's someone here you should meet."

I threaded my way through, was grabbed by the arm and passed through to the centre of a group of about ten men. The three SDF officers, Tom Slaydon, Phillip Rogers, and Tony Morris were all there, flushed and smiling.

"Tell the one about the Irish vet."

"No, not that one! The one about the fellow with

the shits on the train from Broad Street is funnier."

"Oh hell, tell them all."

A drink was jammed into my hand and a cigarette handed to me. I lit it and looked quickly around the group as they were introduced to me. There were two young pink-cheeked subalterns from the regiment garrisoning the island, at the time, some young banking types, some harbour and railway officials, and probably some customs and excise people. We joked and laughed and drank and smoked until about three in the morning. I don't remember buying a drink or smoking one of my own cigarettes, though I must have as my throat was sore in the morning.

I was woken at what seemed like the middle of the night. I had perhaps two or three hours of sleep. I shaved and showered, rushed through the little packing I had to do, and called for a bellhop. We went downstairs together. The bill had already been taken care of by the company. I had some fried eggs and bacon, orange juice, and two large cups of steaming hot and very good coffee, and was ready.

We all met outside in the early morning sun. It was weak and pale and there was some mist hanging about, especially thick below where we were standing. Coming up from the water it was possible to see the three funnels of an old county-class cruiser with her main and foremast sticking up out of the fog. An odd sight.

The car and the bus both arrived at the same time, and this time I was collected by the bus. We drove away down the road into the town, except for those preparing the market stalls, still asleep. We drove for about half an hour and arrived at the airport. Getting off the bus, which had stopped only feet away from the airplane I turned and started to walk towards the plane. It looked so vulnerable in the dawn light, so old and small and rather pathetic.

The water so far below smiled and shined for me that morning. The engine purred and throbbed happily. The air was still, there was no disturbance to the craft as though the elements had heard me worrying about the flight.

We passed to the port side of the island of Pantellaria, a place of evil memories for so many of the Malta convoys, where, from early-morning mists black-topped and yellow-bottomed Heinkels and Stukas rose to take their positions, shake their heads, look around and head for those fragile ships trying to look smaller than they were.

The planes would have stormed down whining and buzzing, to lose their deadly eggs on dapple-grey ships. An occasional dull thud, flash red and yellow, with a second, later, sharp crash as a hit was made, and rusty, slate red hulls saw light for the first time since launched, as they turned slowly over to impossible angles, spilling deck cargo before sinking helplessly into the sea, angry white destroyers busily whipping in and out of their funeral pyres, as terrier dogs around a tree, frustrated at a cat too high to be got at, barking and snapping as if in hopes that the sound and anger will drive away the interloper.

We crossed to the African coast near the Bay of Sollum where I had last been during the war. The chatter and general conversation in the plane had died down as further evidence of the fighting began to show up.

In the desert below, the rusting tanks and armoured cars were noticeable, barely, on the ground due to the sand drifting over. From the air with the sun's position casting shadows, even the smallest protuberance could be seen, such as a radio aerial, perhaps a rusting jerry can, or the remains of a caterpillar track, although its identity and nationality was lost and unimportant now in the common graveyard.

I heard one of the SDF officers say, "Oh, Blimey. Look at the bloody mess there!"

He pointed out the window to the area Montgomery had chosen to meet the final attack by Rommel. In a well dug-in area on the long interrupted ridge he had dug in his tanks: Shermans, Matildas and Grants, his twenty-five pounders, and anti-tank guns, and his British, Indian, Australian, New Zealander, Polish, Free French, and Jewish battalions. We looked down now and held our breath collectively. The sun picked out unmercifully all the horrors of nineteen forty-two.

Some hours later, the plane made its business-like noises before landing. We circled slowly around what appeared to be more desert. As we approached, I was able to see a hut or two, but no other distinct buildings. This would be Wadi Halfa, a name that rang many bells for me. In nineteen thirty-eight I had been much taken by the film "The Four Feathers" made by Alexander Korda. I saw the film seven times and would see it again if given the chance. The film fed my insatiable interest in Africa.

The plane bumped badly. In the afternoon heat the up-currents bent the plane's downward flight severely in all directions. I was feeling queasy when the wheels touched down; however, overall it was a much better landing than the last two. As we taxied down the runway I wiped the sleep from my eyes and the oily sweat from my nose and forehead.

We had been flying for seven hours without any stops and I was feeling jaded. My clothes, made for cold London summers and springs, were too thick, and I was sweating profusely. I felt dirty, my eyes smarted, and my teeth and mouth felt mossy. I looked forward to a long enough stop here that we could get off, brush our mouths out, stretch the legs and belong to the world once again before the last stretch to Khartoum, which was to be another four-hour journey.

The Viking pulled up to the main building. Nearby stood a few petrol tanks and some Nissen huts. The plane stopped and I was first at the door. The steward came aft and opened the door, a small tubular metal staircase on wheels, the usual airport appurtenance, had been wheeled up to the door.

A blast of hot air hit me in the face and body, a solid clang of 120 degrees of heat. This was the North African desert and sun radiated off the myriad stones and granules of sharpened gravel. I caught my breath and steadied myself for I was almost ready to keel over. I was still at the top of the staircase, but no one seemed to be in a hurry, so I didn't hurry either.

The ground stretched away without a break on all four sides that I could see. At my feet the stone and grit were readily discernible but just a few feet away they began to swim and disappear in the heated haze, until, as one looked up towards the horizon, there wasn't really a horizon at all, only a vaguely limpid shimmering area, blue-white at the sky end, and white-yellow at the ground.

After such a long way, I almost expected to be greeted as an adventurous soul. I forgot that to the inhabitants of the country and especially to those whose work takes them for five or more days a week, and for eight hours a day to the environs of the airport or harbour, I am just another blank face, or a page in a passport to be stamped, or a visa to be checked. I was more than disappointed at the lack of fanfare at the various stops we had made so far. This stop was no exception.

We were met by surly soldiers, black with slashed cheeks – their tribal scars it was later explained to me. They wore turbans of khaki cloth in the Indian Army fashion, and khaki drill shirts and shorts, and puttees of the same colour cloth, with open brown sandals. They carried short First World War British Lee-Enfield rifles with the old-fashioned long bayonet attached, which they carried slung over their shoulders. They looked prepared to use them and unpleasant enough. My first impression of the Anglo-Egyptian Sudan was disappointment.

We wandered over to the hut where we were to have our passports checked, under, what I felt rather uncomfortably, was an escort: two soldiers in a casually tense way watching us all very carefully. I got the distinct feeling that they would have loved any one of us to cause some trouble.

We entered the corrugated hut which was surrounded with painted white stones, and I was relieved to see that the officer in charge was English. I had almost forgotten, in my highly charged imagination, this was still a

British-run country, and according to the latest information, likely to remain that way for some time to come. Other than a minor error in some colonial officer's endorsement on one of the pages of my passport we were free and clear.

We all got safely aboard the plane. We were strapped in and ready for take-off. By this time all the romance and excitement had disappeared. I just wanted to get to a place where I could have a cold shower, or bath, put clean clothes on, have something to drink and eat, and go to bed. Once more in this seemingly interminable voyage, we taxied up the strip, revved up engines straining at the leash, released all brakes and were off. We flew into the south and into the ever-increasingly long stretching desert. An uncanny stillness seemed to settle over the country.

Before, in Egypt certainly, there were large areas of desert, but these were interposed with almost equally large tracts of arable ground, green and moist-looking. Now there seemed to be nothing but sand, stone, and every so often, like a belch from the belly of the devil, great outcrops of egg-shaped boulders, one upon the other in some cases so that from the altitude we were flying at they seemed quite high.

I remembered the saying that George had reiterated, "The Arab says that when Allah made the Sudan He laughed." Others call it "the back garden of Allah."

We continued flying steadily south and slightly east, and began to cross the great bend in the Nile where it started to run north in a great sweep, before turning south again. I imagined smudges on the ground to be where Wolseley's expedition to relieve Gordon in eighteen eighty-four was itself forced to form a square and fight off the howling, stabbing, Dervish hordes, where redcoats were for the last time worn, when Gordon had been killed.

It was now beginning to get dark. They say that the African continent gets no twilight to speak of. Well, this is not strictly true of the Sudan. We got a tiny twilight there. The sun would descend towards the horizon at about five or six in the evening and as it got closer to the horizon it moved faster and faster until it would, like a great orange, slip behind the desert rocks. For at least two seconds there would be a faint afterglow, then a velvety darkness that was blue-black and thickly impenetrable.

We began our descent. The instructions were passed to us to prepare for our final landing. This was it. I couldn't believe it. What had begun some three months ago when I had run across the road in front of the Queen's procession to attend an interview had now come to fruition. It all seemed so impossibly long ago. The plane turned gently, as the engines throttled back, and I braced myself once more for the landing.

As the plane circled I looked out of the window to have a look at what was to be my home for the next two years. My heart sank. The sky was clouded over and it was darker because of this, than it would usually have been at this time of early evening. The dusk coloured the desert a grey brown, and I could see patches of water where flooding had obviously occurred, this being the rainy season. It was apparent from the dark thunderheads retreating toward the south, and the dampness of the ground as we got lower, that a heavy storm had just ended, and the whole picture painted was one of gloom and distress.

We landed at the end of a long north-south concreted strip and taxied to the main building. The plane stopped and we climbed out. Walking away from my home of the last two days, I approached the terminal building. It was all very modern, much more so than the one I had left in England. Just before going beneath the balcony surmounting the entrance itself, I looked up to see quite a crowd of greeters who were crying out and yelling at my fellow passengers. I was beginning to feel a little left out when I heard my name called, not loudly, but with a note of authority.

"Payne for the Mercantile Company? Up here! Up here!"

I looked up again and putting on my glasses I found Ronald. He was with a fair-turned-to-grey woman and a tall dark young man. Clearing customs was a matter of minutes and I was soon shaking hands with Ronald, being introduced to his wife Mary, a small but determined Scotswoman, and my future boss Peter Fairchild. He was smart, slick, and not quite a gentleman. He welcomed me with a cold handshake and a smile that ended at his lips. I sensed that I was not quite welcome and wondered why.

"Ah Payne," said Keymer, with his pale blue eyes snapping open and shut, "Welcome to the Sudan."

We walked through the hallway of the airport into the dusk outside. We got into an American Ford custom sedan. Peter got behind the wheel and we drove out onto a narrow blacktop road that pointed straight as an arrow across the horizon.

As the usual pleasantries were exchanged about the trip and so on, I was trying, while being polite, to look out and see what the place was like. I'm not sure what I expected but somehow this was all wrong. It all looked so civilized. We passed a garage lit up with homely reminders to buy Esso petrol, and Pepsi, and Coca-Cola posters, not at all what I expected. It was more like the suburbs of a sandy Golders Green than the edge of a pagan and Muslim Babylon.

We went further into the actual suburbs of the town and as it got darker it became increasingly difficult for me to discern any sort of shape or substance to it. I leaned back into my mind of dreams. This was the city that Gordon defended for some eight months or more. It was the city that attracted all the slavers of yesteryear. This was the capital and sanctuary of the harem begetters, the drug and slave drivers, the central core and intelligence of all that was evil and sordid and exciting at the edge of the eighteenth century as the dullness of civilization and the endless hordes of priests and missionaries drove forward.

We came to a stop in front of an imposing stone and concrete house of two stories, and as I looked upwards from the car window, I noticed a half-storey sort of tower. Little did I know that this was known as the Junior Room and was to be mine for the next six months until someone else went potty or drank too much even for these rules and was ejected back into the world outside.

Ronald said, "Well, Peter Fairchild will introduce you to everyone. Will you have dinner with us at seven-thirty? We dress. Well, good-bye Payne, see you later."

Peter, who had been designated to escort me in,

introduce me around, and see me safely back to the Keymers' by seven-thirty, preceded me into the mess building. We went through some large French doors into the dimly lit dining room. As my eyes got used to the half-light, which was filtering down from a room above, I could see that the table was laid for about eight people.

In the great room were doors opened wide to the night, curtains flapping in the evening breeze, cosily lit from two standing lamps in each of the further corners. There was a gramophone in one corner and in another a white refrigerator. A long comfortable-looking couch took up one full side of the room, and dotted around were several lived-in armchairs. A thick carpet covered most of the red waxed tile floor. The walls were stuccoed white and on the ceiling, suspended and revolving slowly, a long-armed tropical fan. My main interest was in the human occupants of the room who had all stood up with varying expressions on their faces.

The first was a man of about forty in evening dress without a jacket, but with a black cummerbund around his waist. He wore dark horn-rimmed glasses and had a fleshy, pink-jowled look, as from too much good living. This was the company secretary, Tony Braithwaite. His shake was flaccid and uninterested. He sat down before it was decent to do so.

Next in order was a short, fat, rubicund fellow, all broad grin and broad Yorkshire. This was Fred Smith, dishevelled, cheerful, and cynical, and practically upon meeting me he was touching me for a loan.

A foxy-faced, beady-eyed fellow was next. He was dressed still in what was apparently the workday costume:

khaki shorts and shirt open at the neck, long brown socks, and rough shoes nicked and scratched and filmed with dust.

The comparison with the company secretary, polished up as he was, as if for a garden party, was absolute. This was Dennis May, chief electrical engineer. Cockney, cheerful, and a little too friendly. His eyes were also, I noticed, a wee bit on the shifty side.

Eric Tucker was the next and perhaps the most striking of all those I had met already and was to meet. He was dark, with a sallow complexion, closely curled black hair and black-brown eyes. He was very genial.

A little fat man with porcine eyes, very dapper, a little hair left on the pink scalp slicked and combed, brilliantined and brushed to cover the baldness, was next. This was the manager of the garage. The company serviced as well as sold Ford cars, trucks, and tractors. He was buff and hearty and very untrustworthy. This was to be the only correct summing up of character I was to make that evening.

There were two other people there that evening who were field engineers and who were in from their pumping sites out in the desert. They had arrived just before I had, and were already quite drunk beyond the point of introductions. Peter discreetly avoided them for my sake. As he shepherded me to my room I stole a glimpse of them as they sat out on a big sprawling veranda that jutted out over the front door. They were drinking quietly and sadly as they gazed over the parapet into the pale violet afterglow that tinted the distant roofs with the sun's dying light.

Peter showed me to my room in the tower. It was

quite a bit larger than I had expected, and certainly bigger than it had appeared to be from outside. It was furnished sparely, but comfortably. A fairly large and comfortable-looking bed took up most of the room. In one corner next to the bed was a nightstand on which was bedside lamp. The tiled floor had a large throw rug covering about two thirds of the floor space. In another corner, an empty bookcase. The windows were not really windows, but louvered doors, that when pushed open, looked out onto a small and rather frighteningly exposed balcony with a very low parapet, about sixty feet above the ground. I hurriedly closed the doors.

In another corner was an open doorway, or rather an opening, that led into a bathing and washing area, which included a well-appointed, tiled shower stall. It was all like a second-class American motel. Not exactly monastic, but not what you would describe as luxurious. All in all I was more than content.

"I'll pick you up in an hour. Do you have everything? Don't forget we dress, but in the summer you won't be expected to wear a jacket."

I had bought in London a rather spiffy-looking dinner jacket but had entirely forgotten about such things as cummerbunds. Peter told me not to worry, he'd borrow one for me downstairs. He left me to unpack and change.

I got under the shower and relaxed while the tepid water drummed into my head and shoulders, then suddenly got much colder and needled into my scalp, refreshing and rejuvenating me. I heard some movement in the bedroom part and yelled from under the water that I'd be out in a moment, and then switching off the taps, got out, and began to dry, walking out with the towel wrapped around me.

I started to say something and stopped in some astonishment. Leaning over the open drawers of the only other piece of furniture in the room, and neatly putting away my few articles, was a tall, thin, white-clad and turbaned figure, a very black, almost plum-purple colour native. As I came into the room he looked up with a broad smile that split his face in half. He straightened up and stood to attention.

"I am Ali. You Mr. Payne. Salaam allekum, ya." These Arabic words I took to be a greeting and a salute. He place a glass of whiskey and soda on a table and said "Mr. Fairchild's compliments."

I put out my hand to take his in handshake, and he looked at his feet and would not accept my greeting. He shyly looked around the room as if trying to find something else that might attract his attention and so take my mind away from the embarrassing thing I was trying to do.

"Ah, Said has not yet got his evening dress ironed. Ali will fix." (Said meaning "sir" in the colloquialism of the country.)

He flourished my seedy looking jacket and trousers out of the case and began to disappear through the door where he stopped as if in flight and said, "Socks, alright. No holes. An' clean tie. Okay. How about shoes?" He darted again at my case and pulled out both my tie and a rather dilapidated pair of black pumps, and with the air of a conjurer, whisked them up in broad sleeves and disappeared silently down the staircase.

I opened the shutters and let some air in the room. The ceiling fan was whirling around, but was only stirring up the hot air that was already there. I needed some fresh air.

It was quite dark now, and actually fairly cool. The breeze that had come up since nightfall was pleasant and in my situation of undress, positively refreshing. The beads of sweat that had begun to form on my body, dried up, and my flesh and skin began to cool in a most luxurious manner.

I sat by the window and lit a cigarette, picked up the scotch and soda (warm without ice) and sipped slowly, looking out of the window into the darkness. I leaned back and gave myself up to the intensity of the African night.

Gradually I relaxed and became aware of the sounds of the African night. Cicadas starting with a low, barely discernible hum, growing to a screeching hysterical buzz, diminishing, as though in passion spent the insects had flung themselves off some abyss. Myriad other insects were flying about banging into the screens. Drumming sounds were rising and falling in the distance.

It was too theatrical for my first night in Africa. The other strongly resonant predominant sound was that of drums rising and falling, staccato and changing in note and timbre. First a rattle of some insistent message, a pause, then a slow drumming starting in a low off-key beat that suddenly changed to a rhythmic tonal quality. The percussion continued in a hypnotic massage of the brain. These were, I was told later that evening, marriage drums, and I was to get very used to them over the next years as they were a nightly occurrence. A knock at the door interrupted my unplanned reverie.

"Come in."

In walked Ali. "Your suit is ironed and smart. Fit for the King." He smiled.

"Thank you Ali."

"Here also is your tie, and shoes all blacked and shiny."

I got dressed hurriedly, tied the tie, and drank down the last drop of scotch. I remember thinking to myself as I left the room and went downstairs that this is a bit of alright, a servant and all.

I went down the stairs and joined the group in the lounge. They were mostly at one end of the room at the bar. Besides the people I had met earlier, there were some new faces.

"Ah, Payne," this was the dark-visaged Tucker, to be my boss in the morning. "I'd like you to meet Jock MacDonald, our engineer in charge of tractors. He says he works, but we have our suspicions. After all Jock, Fords never break down do they, or don't you believe our own advertising?"

Good-natured banter followed this. Someone asked me what I wanted to drink and I found myself herded onto the veranda with a scotch in my hand. We all found places to sit and stand, and I realised that I was the centre of attraction. In the half hour I had to spare before Fairchild picked me up to take me to Keymer's for dinner, I was expected to tell the boys about England, home and beauty.

"Well, what's it like at home now?"

Of course I knew now that I was expected to give a long and detailed account about the girls, the theatre, the latest scandal, songs, and cricket scores, also of course the jokes. These I could manage and reeled off several in quick succession. Thank God for George Price. My ignorance about all the other subjects didn't seem to matter as much.

When the laughter faded they began to ask for more funny stories. I was now, after several drinks and many stories, beginning to enjoy myself, but knew, looking at my watch, that Peter would be arriving any minute. We had just ordered another round of drinks, as Fred Smith had warned me that the whiskey did not exactly flow freely at Keymer's and that I had better stock up here, when in trotted Peter.

"Well, we'd better get cracking. Keymer's a stickler for punctuality."

His haste to leave did not prevent him from downing a large scotch and soda in one gulping drink. He had also learned from experience about the dry qualities of the forthcoming evening. We went downstairs and entered a Ford saloon car. In it was Peter's wife. She was an Italian-Maltese girl, dark, large, and charming who immediately put me at ease. Where Peter was inclined to be stuffy, she was utterly disarming, loquacious where Peter was somewhat succinct, and friendly when he seemed reserved.

We drove through the quiet dark streets, black topped with sandy edges, heavily treed along the sides, with dark mysterious front gardens.

We turned off what seemed to be the main road and drove up along the drive, swung again to the left, and came to a halt. Immediately, as the engine was switched off the wind sound made by the car's movement stopped and I was aware of the insects around me again. They were louder. It seemed as though all the insects in Christendom were exaggerated in size and were pressing on the window glass trying to get in.

As I opened the door I felt a wash of soft brushing creatures against my face and hands. The sensation was faintly disgusting and I was relieved when a large light was switched on to our right, illuminating a gateway set into the wall surrounding an extensive-looking estate, and drawing the attention of all these nocturnal flying objects toward it, although Peter and Sarah did not seem to notice.

Peter went up to the gate and said something to a white-dressed figure barely discernible in the half-light. The figure bowed gravely and replied by opening the door. We walked up a long path preceded by this person, obviously quite old and bent. The path was as a tunnel, with high bushes that had conspired to meet overhead. It was pitch black except for an occasional weak electrical light.

We came out upon an expanse of close-trimmed grass, upon which tables and chairs had been placed here and there. A standing lamp had been situated to give a faltering light to the occasion. The lights were practically all covered with bugs. We came a stop, me feeling a little as Stanley must have upon descrying the clearing in which he knew would be Livingstone's tent.

"What's up?" I asked Peter.

"Shhh, here comes Keymer now!"

This was my third sight and meeting with Ronald Keymer, Officer of the Most Excellent Order of the British Empire, Military Class. The last time had been in London when he yawned in my face and when I had formed a snap opinion of him which was not complimentary. It had not occurred to me at the time that this Englishman was not at home in England.

He was truly at home here, surrounded by the exoticisms that seem to sit so well with certain Anglo-Saxon types. Perhaps it was his dinner wear, which was conservative to the polished boots, but with an air of rakehell central tropic attached to him. Perhaps it was in the way he carried himself, the tone of voice, or the mannerisms of gesture and glance of ownership. Certainly a combination of all increased his stature. Ronald was very much at home here.

"Yes, yes. Payne our new man. Ah, Fairchild and Sarah. Ah, jolly good. Won't you sit down?" He indicated wicker armchairs that were set around under jacaranda trees and flowering jasmine and honeysuckle.

"Mary will be out in a moment or two."

He settled us all down, and like a dog circling around and sniffing before settling, made several vaguely nervous turns around us all before unwinding some six plus feet into a chair that looked much too small to hold him.

"Ah Payne, do you drink?" He gave me a piercing, and I thought, rather disapproving look as though daring me to admit to this shocking weakness.

I remembered what the boys had told me and what Peter himself had mentioned, but did so badly feel like one that it didn't take too much courage to say rather hypocritically "a very weak whiskey and water."

"Yes, yes. Water. Yes. By all means, water. A capital suggestion." A look half craft and half lunatic crossed his face and he braced himself in the chair, his knuckles whitening as though in a superhuman effort to place

141

himself under control. A gasp and his eyes closed tightly for a second or two.

I was alarmed, and looked around at the others for suggestion. They were interestedly gazing at a prematurely darkening sky. I looked back hurriedly at Keymer and instead of, as I had expected, an apoplectic fit being thrown, he was calmly eyeing me as though nothing had happened.

"And you, Peter and Sarah?" transferring a now cold and baleful stare at my companions.

"That sounds fine sir, I think I'll join you."

With this he braced himself again, strained his body half out of the chair, gripping the arms firmly, screwed his eyes tightly shut, and with a voice that started as a grumble from his nethermost depths and emerged a veritable howl, he shouted with great resonance and fury as though commanding the legions of hell to do his bidding.

"MOHAMMED!" I almost leaped out of my chair with fright and the cigarette I had just lit, flew out of my hand and lay burning on the ground. I looked again at Peter and Sarah and they were absently contemplating their fingernails. I quickly picked up the cigarette and, expectantly wondering what was to come next, looked up again to Keymer. He was smiling benevolently at me.

"Mohammed is rather old and inclined to deafness you know. Ought to let him go, but all you can get now are missionary trained people who are most unsatisfactory. Ah, there you are Mohammed."

At this moment, out of the darkest shadows on the lawn, silently crept a most sinister figure. He looked to be conservatively about a hundred years old, dressed entirely in the native Sudanese djellaba, a floor length garment of white cotton, gathered in at the waist with a green waistband. He also wore a white turban, and sandals on the feet.

"Yes, yes, Mohammed." Ronald seemed then to float into another world. He stared at the servant as though seeing him for the first time, wrinkling his brow as though in a desperate attempt to collect his thoughts and recognize this man. He then glowered at Peter and Sarah, turned to me and said in a high pitched voice, "I understand that you can speak several languages. Trilingual in fact."

As I was stammering my protestations of this amount of knowledge, I heard out of the corner of my ear, Peter instructing the wrinkled retainer as to our wishes drink-wise. The servant padded silently into the shadows and disappeared as mysteriously as he had arrived.

"No, no Payne, you can't be modest. I like modesty, naturally, but one can overdo it, can't one? Italian mother. Aye, I know." A roguish gleam came into his eye, a most unsuitable expression for him as it gave him the appearance of an aged llama winking at the feeders in the zoo.

"Well, sir..." I started.

"No, you must always be proud of the Italian blood. Didn't do too well in the last lot, but jolly good music, lovely climate, and really the best ship architects going. Upon my soul. Splendid, splendid."

"Ah, where the devil did that come from?" as a glass of whiskey was whisked quietly and efficiently into his hand. "Ah Payne got one too. Mohammed, wonderful chap. Reads the mind, really quite irreplaceable."

We sipped. It was a much stronger drink than I had been led to expect.

"So Payne, we sail here, have a lovely little Butterfly. Hope you'll use it as often as you like."

At about this point, Mary, his little Scottish wife, came out the house and joined us. She was a charming, small woman with a mind of her own. She was friendly in a withdrawn way and I never really ever got to know her. We chatted of this and that, without any meaningful depth and at an obviously pre-arranged signal from Ronald, the ancient servant reappeared to announce that dinner was ready.

We trooped into the house. This building, like the one that we were living in, was about twenty or thirty years old. The architecture was similar, in that the layout was constructed to obtain maximum effects from the airs coursing about, and was arranged to catch and channel these breezes to their best effect.

The house was made of brick and stucco, single storied, and arranged in the shape of an "L." All the floors were of red tile, cool-looking and cold to the touch. The inside walls were an off-white colour and rough in appearance. The living room we walked through on our way to the dining room was furnished in a mixed up way. There were some good English pieces of mahogany and walnut, well waxed and rubbed, and obviously taken care of, one desk that looked Queen Anne-ish, an Oriental rug of some size that must have been very expensive, bookcases overflowing with books, some standing lamps, potted plants, and a variety of pictures of all sorts covered all four walls. A comfortable room of some confident taste, and from the look of the chintz-covered sofa and chairs, a much-lived-in room.

The way into the dining room was through a pair of handsome French doors. Inside there was placed a long table of mahogany, laid for the evening's meal, with lace and cut glass and good dinnerware. There were candles held in heavy silver sconces. Bowls of fruit, *and* decanters of wine were placed at intervals. I began to cheer up. It wasn't going to be as bad as I thought it was going to be.

The dinner began with a most thought-provoking soup called "ful sudani." It was made of peanuts, cream, eggs and water. It was a delicious local dish.

After dinner Keymer hospitably passed round a box of cigarettes that were so old that the match, put up to the end, caused the dried up tobacco to burn at a furious pace, leaving about a half inch of fag in the fingers. After some desultory conversation, we all rose and entered the drawing room, sat around on deep chairs, and drank one glass of brandy each. After my long flight and late hours I was in danger of dropping off to sleep in the middle of my new chief s dissertations, and had from time to time to shake my head to realise where I was.

At last it was time to leave, and I witnessed a ritual that was to become familiar to me over the years I would spend in this country and in the company of Mr. and Mrs. Keymer. A waiter, a younger one this time, walked in bearing a large silver tray upon which were laid some glasses and a large glass carafe of water. Almost as in a ceremony that held some religious meaning, the glasses were artfully filled and passed around to the guests who all sipped or took a long swallow according to their needs and experience. Upon these ablutions being performed, Keymer got up and looked vaguely out of the window. This was the dismissal. First Peter then Sarah stood up. I sat in some bewilderment for a moment or two, then realizing the significance of the ritual, rose also.

"Well it was kind of you to come. I do hope we shall see each other again soon."

"Thank you sir," I said, "for a lovely dinner. It was most kind."

We were shepherded out by the old servant who had reappeared. As we walked back down the path, now lit by a very bright moon casting enormous slanting black and white shadows, I thought of the peculiarity of the evening's farewell. It was as though I had been an accidental guest, someone that had been forced unavoidably on them for the meal only, and that it had been with relief that they had got rid of me. No mention had been made of the job or of having met me in London for the interview. It was really as though we had never met before and were completely and totally strangers, and would, as far as Keymer was concerned, remain so. Peter dropped me off at the mess after a silent drive, except for his wife's chattering. I found my way to bed and slept soundly.

I was awake very early next morning. Peter had told me of the strange and early hours they kept for work to avoid the midday and afternoon heat. It was about five-thirty when I got out of bed and showered in the convenient stall attached to my bedroom. After the bath I went over to the shuttered windows, opened them, and looked out...

This was my first view of Khartoum, the city of so

much magic and promise. My first impression as the sun came up over the trees, was of many white and yellow rooftops, flat and shadowed by the retaining walls surrounding their tops, apparently made of mud, bricks, and stucco.

Interspersed between the houses and huts were many trees, a dark dusty green, bushes and shrubs proliferating in and around the buildings, giving an impression of a town about to be strangled by undergrowth. In all directions, cutting through the houses and greenery, were roads, surfaced in some of the major cases, with tarmac, in others with dust and gravel, all the roads cutting through each other in the design laid down by Sir Herbert Kitchener in the form of a Union Jack. This also, it was said, made it easy to control in case of trouble. A machine gun at the crossovers could control all eight arms at will.

At this early hour it was still fairly cool, though the sun's rays could be felt already and promised another scorching day out of the pale dusty blue sky. A faint, pale, golden haze hung low over the whole town. The dust kicked up from the previous day had not yet dispelled in the still air. Scents of sweet jasmine and honeysuckle lay heavily and drowsily around.

I went down to the dining room, which, at six-thirty was already full of eating figures. An empty seat was available. Rapid and garbled introductions were made between gulped mouthfuls of eggs and porridge. I sat down and looked around me. The amount of food laid on the table was fantastic. There were plates piled with hard and soft boiled eggs, plates lay there with sheaves of hot crisp bacon, dishes of fried bread and tomatoes, and deep china bowls filled to the brim with bubbling porridge kept warm by a spirit flame underneath. On another, plates with piles of toast, dishes in between with strawberry jam, marmalade of three kinds: orange, lime, and grapefruit, and practically at each elbow, pots of coffee, sending into the air clouds of heavily scented steaming billows of that lovely, appetizing, roasted brew. I tucked in with a will after my rather stringent breakfast years of post-war England.

Afterwards, with a third cup of coffee with milk, I lit a luxurious cigarette, and sat back. The servants busied themselves about clearing the table, and before starting off to the office, Eric and I were left alone together.

"Finish your coffee and we'll go. You will meet your staff today."

"Fine. I'm ready."

"Let's go then."

I stubbed out my cigarette and got up. Like all the others, I was dressed that morning in the Sudan's summer uniform: khaki shorts, long cream-coloured woollen socks, vyella shirt buttoned and with a tie, and brown suede desert boots. I was still a little self-conscious about my skinny legs, but no one made any comment, so I was beginning to feel a little more comfortable.

We went out of the cool tiled room and walked out into blinding white glare of the sun. Eric had his company car parked nearby. It was, as all the cars were, a Ford, the company having the agency to sell these in the Sudan. Eric's was a nineteen fifty-three French Vedette, a dark green vicious-looking, high-powered beast with fat desert balloon tires.

We got in and drove down to the centre of town where the offices were. We drove down streets with hard dirt surfaces, raising clouds of dust in our path. Eric told me that the rains were expected any moment, this being the month of July. They had already had their main rainfall for April, then a hot dry spell, then usually a little more, at least sufficient to lay the dust for a while.

Oleander trees hung overhead as we rode through the outskirts of town. Heavy-laden trees of prickly yellow acacia, the bush tree of Central Africa, geraniums, and nasturtiums, grew wild climbing and creeping over house walls and roofs. Luxuriant growths of every conceivable tropical and sub-tropical flower and plant grew and thrived under and in spite of the driving beating sun. We came to a square in the centre of town – drove around it passing the market stalls. We were surrounded by traffic of cars, horse-driven carriages, and bicyclists on every hand, all fighting and arguing for some space in the road.

On each side as we passed, rose two and sometimes three-storey buildings, obviously government offices, white and tan and yellow, with large and imposing windows like medieval arrow slots, mauve and purple-shadowed from the sun. At each entrance, lines of natives standing as in a queue, waiting for God-knows-what down a palm-lined double-laned boulevard, the centre a grass plot planted with date palms.

Further on, on one side, our right, the river, was the Blue Nile – one of Gordon's natural bastions in the siege of eighteen eighty-four, running fast and clear, swimmable, unlike the White, which was really brown and sluggish. On our left the government house. Then the statue of

Kitchener, the reputed saviour of the Sudan, who, some years later, defeated the Dervish army just a mile or so away across the river at Omdurman, the largest native city in the world, a thriving hive of human comings and goings, seething with life and death, disease and new birth.

After the rains the Blue Nile was up high, and we passed the Grand Hotel with its annex bobbing up and down on its mooring. Gordon's gunboat "The Bordein" was perhaps the most exotic and glamorous of all the world's hotel extensions. And there was Gordon, still up there in bronze, quietly and doggedly riding his camel into one more slave camp, walking stick held up surreally as in baptism rather than in threat, but now with pigeons and doves nesting in his tarboosh. Perhaps he would have liked that.

The head office of the Sudan Mercantile Company Motors Khartoum and Engineers Company was situated facing one of the large grassed squares of the central city. Made of brick and concrete and stuccoed over, it was block shaped and narrow-windowed, each opening shuttered with dark green steel jalousies. These were convenient for keeping the mid-afternoon sun out.

Eric parked the car around the side of the building and immediately a little plum-black man in voluminous white clothes ran up and starting to polish and water it. We went into the office building. Almost at once we were stopped and I was introduced to a little bird-like man, name of Bugler. He jerked around nervously as he talked animatedly, looking at Eric and then at me. He was from the Midlands. He had sheafs of paper under his arms and seemed frightfully important.

Afterwards, Eric told me to watch him as he was apparently terribly untrustworthy and read one's private mail. Eric had apparently got fed up with John Bugler's habit of going through the offices, reading the private and sometimes confidential mail that might be on his desk, and had once printed on a large sheet of paper, "Mind your own bloody business, Bugler!" and put it under the top sheet of paper on the pile. Bugler had avoided Eric's eyes and presence for some time after that.

"These are the small parts stores, Ted," Eric said, pointing to a long row of counters on one side of the main hall, a hall or foyer that soared about thirty feet up to the ceiling, in the centre of which was an old horizontal diesel engine, beautifully polished and, it was said, capable of snorting and wheezing into action given an injection of oil and flame. The hall was painted a pale cool green colour. This, with the waxed and polished tile floor which was of an ochre colour, gave a feeling of coolness and permanent stability, an oasis within the hot surround of the red, white, and yellow, and green, of the turmoil without.

"This is Mr. Payne. Ted, this is Ali Effendi, the chief storekeeper." We shook hands.

With a sharp white smile, eyes intelligent, neat, and personable, "Welcome Mr. Payne, ya Said."

"How do you do?" I answered lamely. I was determined to learn the language.

We went along rows and rows of neatly stacked and card-indexed steel parts, placed on shelves all ready to be removed and placed into faltering pumps and diesel engines, cotton milling machines, steam and motor road rollers, stern-wheeled paddle steamers, corn grinding machines, and tractors and asphalt-layers. Dark corridors of gleaming parts wrapped, each one in slightly greasy but dustless waxed paper. I was very impressed.

We left the store and walked over to what was to be my office. A tall door set in the green wall, within which, brass with EXECUTIVE ENGINEER, MR. E. A. PAYNE glistening newly. I pretended nonchalance. We walked inside, where sitting was a very little black man with a cheerful face who at once jumped up and stood to attention. Beside him was a young, much blacker youth, who, nervously, seeing his senior's example, almost fell over trying to outdo him in rigidity and speed.

"Ted, this is your right-hand man," indicating the older man, "Ezzel Din Effendi El Tayeb."

Ezzel Din beamed at this introduction. I immediately took a great liking towards him.

"Fuddle Mr. Payne, ya Said. Welcome to Mercantile." Fuddle, I learned later, was the expression used to indicate that one was to make oneself at home, a most winsome form of greeting I thought. The other boy was one Awad, a handsome little fellow who seemed honest, unassuming, fearless, and full of fun.

Ezzel Din was of the old school who believed in the British rule of benevolent undertaking, trusted the English implicitly, and would die for nothing else than for loyalty to the white king or queen who he had never, or would never see. His grandfather had fought mine at Omdurman sixty years prior. Ezzel Din later protected me when things went wrong, much in the fashion of the sergeant major trying to cover up for his beloved but stupid officer.

His face was really quite extraordinary. At birth his tribe decreed mutilation of the face, a fairly common ritual amongst the central and southern Nilotic groups. As an infant emerged from the mother's body, the elders of the clan would ceremoniously take the child and in its forehead embed small pieces of gravel. In the cheeks incisions were made. These, at the time, were of a minor nature, but as the head grew larger, the scars and indentations grew along with the enlargement of the general parts.

My nemesis, I was to discover, was the manager of the Khartoum Company. This was one Latimer, a cold fish Baptist type, non-conformist, teetotaller, thin of lip, long of nose, and steely of eye. He disapproved of me from the beginning and the feeling was mutually strong. I really should have had nothing to do with him, but the first job I had was loosely connected with his side of the business.

I was seconded as it were, to his department, as a sort of training period. I was asked if I would take over the job of checking a large consignment of steelwork arrived from England some six months or so before, and only now to be used for the construction of some new showrooms for our motor company. The pile of iron was lying in some obscure empty lot on the south side of Khartoum.

I was supposed to hire the local natives, "pick them out and set them to work." My job was to stand on a small mound of earth and check off every nut, bolt, and girder as they carried these items past me and laid them out on a pile on the other side of the yard.

The heat was fantastic. To start with, I had a terrible job hiring the help. Most of them argued all sorts of excuses as to why they should be in some sort of advisory or supervisory capacity; very few of them actually wanted or were willing to carry things. I didn't blame them. We finally got things sorted out, me with my Egyptian assistant. (We were in a strange position apropos the Egyptians in this country, this being the Anglo Egyptian Sudan as formed in eighteen ninety-eight but really run by the British).

We spent about three days in the grilling sun, checking and carrying, counting and piling, until I was satisfied that everything was in order with the exception of one minor bag of nuts and bolts, and on this premise I made my report in quadruplicate. Original to Keymer, copies to Motors Co. first, and secondarily to Khartoum Co. London office, and one for the file.

The second copy was my mistake. The head of Khartoum Co. was this Latimer. Between the time that he received my minute concerning the missing bag, and the time that he set up court martial proceedings for my laxity, I had already sent an order to England, to the factory, ordering a duplicate. That was my second error.

"How dare you sir?" was the opening broadside. "How dare you take it upon yourself to order more spare parts without first checking with me?"

"But I didn't think it was that important."

"Didn't think that important? Where do you think you are, the bargain basement of Selfridges? These items cost money. Money, do you understand? Pounds, shillings, and pence. You young pups come out from England and think you can run things into the ground."

He was working himself up into a frenzy of unbelievable proportions. I began to get quite alarmed.

Perhaps he was going to become violent. I had heard of these tempers of the colonials who had spent all their lives under tropical suns, drinking, and so on. But Latimer didn't drink. What was I to do?

He gripped the sides of his office chair in an effort at control. Quite calmly and quietly he spoke between his teeth, looking not at me but out the window.

"You will cancel that letter to London and you will go back to the yard where the steelwork is, and you will recheck every item once more and report back to me. Good day sir."

My sympathetic friends advised me to do exactly what he said. I faced the next morning with a hangover. In a rather bewildered state of mind I went through the same procedures, hiring the vagrant workers with my foreman who looked upon the whole project sour-eyed. We had two bad accidents that first day, a mashed foot and a bad laceration of the face, both when large and very heavy pieces of steelwork escaped their moorings and came crashing down with sickening thuds on my poor boys' parts.

The day was terribly hot and never seemed to end. There was no shade on this yard and I felt constrained out of pity to help cart and carry.

By nightfall I was in a state of nervous and physical exhaustion, and was ready to tell Latimer where he could stick his nuts and bolts. I drove back to the mess in the car supplied, and arrived in a mucky sweat. Dinner had already been laid and served, and by most of the house, eaten and digested. My meal was on a hotplate. I picked at it indifferently in the half darkness, fuming to myself. I didn't want to unload myself so soon upon my fellow messmates, but had somehow to find some consolation for all my real or imagined injustices. I laid down knife and fork and dragged myself upstairs. At least I needed a drink.

There were only the two field engineers sitting in the lounge. The record player was switched on and they were both dreamily and drunkenly listening to Rosemary Clooney. They didn't even look up as I came in and went over to the bar to make myself one and sign the chit. Drinking after hours in the mess bar was on the honour system. If you wanted a drink after the servants had gone to bed, you helped yourself and signed out what you had on a pad. I slumped down in one of the chairs and moodily sipped the warm whiskey.

"What's up Ted?"

I opened my eyes. "What?" I said.

"What's up Ted?" It was one of the field men.

"Well I'm in a mess."

In a moment of mental weakness I poured out my troubles to the kindly and liberally flushed face of the stranger. He listened sympathetically nodding now and again in understanding of some of the more pointed parts of my tale.

"Well, we know what you're talking about, that old bastard doesn't have the sense to come inside when it's raining. What you need is another drink. Let's all go down to the Gordon!" This was a local cabaret, the only one I might add.

"Now that's a good idea," said Jim Bradley, obviously the leader in the group. A big hulking fellow with the kind of face that has nothing to lose. Cauliflower ears, broken nose, and scarred in several different directions across the face – a very tough character. We drank down the remains of our whiskeys and left down the stairs into the moonlit courtyard where the cars were parked.

We all got into one car, Jim's, an old Ford. It was in bad shape, clouds of oil smoke billowed out behind us as we broke the silent white night with bellowing engine and voices raised, though in unison but not in tune, while disturbed figures dashed out behind us to stare after us in quiet bewilderment and silent irritation. We threaded our way through the damp cool evening, through the drugged brown streets, backwards and forwards, mosques praying against the light sky. Here and there a black face, white-teethed, white-gowned figure, would detach itself from the shadows to stare in wonder as we groaned and belched by. Otherwise it was as silent as the desert.

We came finally to a dark wide street lined with rotting palms. A dog snapped and growled and I could see a deep ditch as I opened the car door. On my right a minaret was outlined against the sky above a group of low black buildings. I could hear above the quiet hum of the sleeping city, music, zithers and drums, and a wailing high-pitched singing.

"Here we are," said Jim.

"Let's go and see the girls. They say there's a good group tonight."

We walked through the heavy full-scented night and approached a dimly lit archway. We went through and found ourselves in a brightly lit foyer – it was still out of doors but heavily illuminated and guarded.

Several dubious-looking locals in a common

uniform stood around and examined us. At a small black table sat a fat Levantine girl. She asked for money in exchange for which we were given tickets. Another dark tree and plant-lined corridor, then more brightness and here we were in the bar of the famous Gordon Cabaret.

The arrangement was circular, around a small dance floor tiled in shiny waxed red. On all the tables sat a bowl of fresh flowers and a candle or two set in a bottle. The residue of a thousand dead ones laid in swirls and lines of cold wax around the base. Above the head, as one sat down, were the bending swaying leaves of trees, set and planted in earthen areas around here and there. Entwined in the branches, myriad fairy lights, yellow and white, blinked and stuttered as the evening breeze waved them about, rattling and clinking against the leaves and branches.

At one side of the circle was set a low stage, perhaps a foot, no more, above the dance floor. To one side, a roofed-over loggia, trellised and intertwined with honeysuckle, wild roses, and jasmine. Beneath and to the rear of this construction, barely seen save for the dim golden lights, was the bar – the haven of the British bachelor, where, at a heavily varnished African mahogany slab of elephantine proportions, one might lean, stand, or sit, buy drinks for the girls before they joined the really paying customers, swap stories, listen to tales of the interior from hoary white hunters, with the deliciously added feeling of knowing that this interior is only some five hundred miles as the crow flies from where you're sitting and sipping your gin and tonic.

That first night I met two of the girls. I was in a highly excited state of mind and ready for practically anything. I had been out almost a week and was already an old African hand. The first girl was an Abyssinian. She was beautifully dark, sinuous and lithe. She was scarred from ancient rituals, short-haired, with teeth that were sharpened almost to points. With the surrounding atmosphere, her flashing eyes and taloned fingers in my hair, she was an object of succulent desire.

I can't remember exactly what happened, but apparently I made a disparaging remark about her Emperor Sellassie, and she flew across the room to fasten those little sharp white teeth in my cheek. The force sent me flying across the bar with her still attached, much in the manner of a Staffordshire terrier at the threat of a bear. We were finally detached from each other and she was dragged off swearing more violence to come. At once horrified and shook up, it was several gins later that I was able to take an interest in the later proceedings.

We all went out and took a table, ordered another bottle of Johnny Walker Red Label and sat back to watch the show. This was a dancing group recruited in Berlin, Athens, Rome, and Ankara – clumsy and graceless in retrospect. But that night they possessed all the beauty and fluidity of motion of a Russian ballet. Coarse farmer girls from the back hills of Turkey and the Balkans seemed possessed with the delicacy and liquid character of a Fonteyn. Several drinks and many performances later I was supported back to the car and driven, singing and shouting, back to the mess. My room being on the top level, it was required that I be escorted and put to bed.

On to the office by about seven thirty, where the

first order of day was to have the nearest bring coffee. This was not coffee as the European or American thinks of coffee, this was the strong syrupy brew recognised by Greeks and Arabs as the drink of the Gods. Hot, in small demitasse cups, served with a carafe of water. Sweet, black, and with dregs that tried to filter past the teeth when the last mouthful was swallowed. Reviving and delicious once one had got used to it. It was definitely an acquired taste.

Files would be brought in for the day's work. The girls didn't start until eight o'clock so this was the period when one started to appraise what one was to do to prepare for the correspondence that would have to be written to London and to the various prospective clients in the country who might be requiring quotations on anything from a thousand-pound pumping site erection, to a corn grinder, to a Vickers Armstrong tractor built like a tank, to a diesel-engined road roller.

We chatted and gossiped, Ezzel Din and I and Awad, and visited back and forth with other members of the company, English, Arab, and Sudani. At eight-thirty we returned to the mess for breakfast, a rest of a few minutes, after, a smoke and an informal meeting between all the junior staff followed, then we returned to the office.

The time between nine and twelve was filled with meeting prospective and existing clients, dealing with complaints, soothing ruffled feathers, explaining why the spare parts needed had not arrived, checking on shipments from the Red Sea port of entry, examining stores and checking inventories, and settling a squabble between two clerks with equal grievances.

We broke up for lunch, then spent an afternoon in

the always-astounding heat. At night, after supper, we would one by one quietly drift off to our rooms, the shutters of which would have been pulled closed earlier by our servants so that some coolness would have been retained. The ceiling fan would have been switched on to a slow speed.

It would not take long to drift off into a heavy sleep; the beer and hot food relaxed our muscles and nerves. The time from two to four seemed seconds, when we would again be shaken awake by our servants with a cup of tea, sip this in a state of heavy drowsiness, and stagger into the shower to wake up under the icy needles of water. Into clean long trousers or shorts, shirt, and off to the office again for two more hours of solitary study and preparation for the day.

Often we would go to one of the half-dozen or so open-air cinemas, the Blue Nile, the Wadatania, of which there were three, the one in Khartoum north, the one downtown, and the one in the western part of town. These places, where the latest Hollywood movies were shown, were a source of much pleasure and entertainment to us and to the vast local audience. Attending a show in the middle of the rainy season and the simultaneous sandstorm season was an experience I'm sure would have made the producers proud of their efforts on the various sagas we saw, had they seen the patience and stubbornness with which we sat through blinding dust and sand, torrential rains and wind high on the Beaufort scale, so that we would get our value for the piastre paid.

Saturdays we worked until noon, and of course

Sundays were set aside for much entertaining. There were not many Sundays that went by without having several parties to attend, many that we ourselves would put on at the mess. Jock and I were the social convenors. We arranged and put on the first big party the Mercantile Company had in fifty years. We sent out the invitations. As many girls as we could muster were asked, English, Greek, Jewish, Italian, Armenian, Arabic, French, and Syrian. We had a bar constructed and placed on the flat roof behind the mess. Potted plants of various sizes and types were purchased and set around in an attractive way. On the walls and in niches in and around the lounge area coloured fairy lights were suspended.

Our waiters were resplendent in sparkling white with green cummerbunds, and turbans. Ali, the senior, was placed at the door to welcome arrivals and advise the parking of cars. We asked everyone of any importance from the Governor General to the wealthiest landowner in the country. Crates of scotch, gin, and champagne were on hand, soft drinks for the Muslims, food from hors d'oeuvres to chicken, turkey, sides of ham and beef, vegetables of all description – all was ready.

At eight, the first guests arrived and they didn't stop coming until midnight, when the party was in full swing. The crush outside to park cars was so intense that the police were called out to secure the peace. I went out on the upper roof at one time to get some air and as far as the eye could see down the street were cars and people struggling to get in. It was a fantastic success and was to set the pattern for parties held later both in our mess and in many others. Perhaps a good five-hundred people attended that were countable because we knew them. Goodness knows how many uninvited guests there must have been.

The week following the party I was to set out on my first trek with Eric along with one servant named Mohammed. We were to do a four-hundred mile swan down to the pumping sites of Shabluka and Merowe. We started at the crack of dawn Tuesday, a trip that would normally take three days and nights not counting the stops for sleep at each station and every refreshment in between.

We left Khartoum, the pearly African dawn seeping over the horizon. Once out of the suburbs and bumping at sixty down a rutted washboard road, there was nothing to obscure the view to the edge of land in any of four directions and I was amazed at my first sight of the great orange tinted sun climbing above the earth's perimeter. I had seen this at sea during the war, but somehow over the hard ground the immensity of the sun seemed more awesome than on the ocean.

Eric and all the old hands had a theory, which was probably right, that the only way to drive on these roads, seamed hard after the rains had come and gone, was to drive like mad down them. If you went slowly your teeth were shaken loose from the gums. However there was a feeling of some insecurity fishtailing across the desert at a very high rate of speed and passing overturned buses wheels spinning slowly, looking like massive turtles turned on their backs and all surrounded by their passengers yelling and cursing us as we swept by.

"No good to stop," said Eric, "they would all want to get onboard and we'd be swamped. There'll be another bus along with spare parts in a few hours."

We drifted on further south and the first excitement began to fade. We had been driving now for some six hours and I was tired, hot, dusty, and thirsty. It was now about midday and nothing in any direction was to be seen. The Hollywood version of the desert is far from the truth. In reality the desert is flat, hard, mostly made up of volcanic gravel and rock, occasionally a soft spot of deep sand, but mostly sand mixed with gravel and stones. Now and again a scrubby acacia bush with the odd goat chewing the upper leaves, but otherwise nothing as far as the eye can see. This is the really frightening thing about the desert: hardly any discernible living things.

We stopped for a change of drivers and a stretch, and I was shocked by the utter silence that encompassed us. The whole land around seemed to sigh in its contented air of having absolute mastery over such puny beings as us. In the distance we would sometimes see the infamous shimmering mirage, not as the stories or movies say, not a castle or oasis or wobbling houri, but great sheets of shiny shimmering water, as though there were some great lake or inner sea just a short drive away. Of course, as one approached it gradually disappeared from sight.

It was now mid-afternoon and hotter than hell. We had the doors of the Land Rover latched forwards, open to their full extent, and had suspended outside our goatskin bags of water for the cool air to catch and bead with tears. In the back of the lurching bumping car Mohammed lay snoring, his pink-palmed hands turned upwards as in supplication, his toes and feet grasping our one rifle, his pride and joy, only to be used in the direst extremities, when starving or in danger from desert bandits who might take a fancy to our wristwatches.

As far as shooting food was concerned, I hadn't even seen a scorpion yet. Where were all the wild animals of the continent I'd been told about? The drumming of the engine and sonorous whine of the transmission, together with the heat and lulling sway and swoop of the reverse motion eventually put me into a dream-filled intermittent doze, and when I awoke we were stopped in a silent void, a dark and starless gloom, and with a start I realised that I was alone.

I leaped up and out of the car, looking around with the tingling sensation of fear and the taste of iron in my mouth. Where in hell were they?

Ah, a feeling of relief at seeing the two shadowy forms of Eric and Mohammed huddled together trying to light a fire. I was so relieved as I approached them.

"God, you gave me a bloody fright."

"Oh, sorry," said Eric. "You were sleeping so soundly we hated to wake you."

Mohammed chuckled and went about his business, furtively looking at me then at Eric, and muttering smilingly to himself. I felt very silly and amateurish. In very short order Mohammed had a two-man tent up, a washbasin, a table, and a brisk fire burning with various pots cooking and bubbling with some stew made from odd cans he produced from his store in the back of the Rover.

It was only then that I realised that it was not as dark as I had thought and was in fact, upon looking at my watch, only about seven-thirty. This was the illusion brought about by dropping off to sleep at high bright noon and waking in the evening and to the nonexistent African twilight. One moment it was light, the next dark. I was to have this odd experience many more times during my time in the bush.

I threw some cool water into my face and washed the dust off my hands, using the canvas washbasin erected for the purpose, wiping my hands, and walking back to the fire. I realised all of a sudden something else odd about the Central African plateau: it got bloody cold when the sun went down.

I sat down in the folding chair near the fire and looked out across the desert. In the distance the afterglow was causing a pink glow over one side of some strange rocky tumbled hills. In the middle distance on one side they were quite black, on the other, this peculiar salmon pink colour. In the far distance the desert stretched grey and foreboding in the direction that we were to take in the morning. I shivered.

"Care for a quick one before dinner?"
It was Eric with a bottle in one hand and two dusty glasses in the other.

"You bet." I said. "I'm dying for one, or for that matter, several."

"Fine." He laughed and sat in the other chair holding the two glasses in hand. He slopped them full of whiskey and handed me one. I drank a gulp and the fire coursed down, choking and marvellous. I sat back and lit a fag, relaxing and stretching.

While I sipped and dragged I listened to Eric telling me about the country we were to visit. We would, in the next fifty miles, leave the rough desert road such as it was, and strike out across virtually trackless ground. Here we would depend upon the compass and stars for our position, using celestial navigation, much in the manner of mariners of old. If we ran out of food we had our rifle, and the country, though not abounding in game, was fairly well inhabited by gazelle and desert deer.

Water of course could be a problem. Naturally all we had to do if in trouble was head east and we would eventually hit the Nile, but it was possible to run out of petrol, have mechanical trouble, or just get lost and run around in circles following one's own track. The compass might go awry or be dropped, or the locals might get upset. All sorts of possibilities could have occurred and I was glad to see Eric's calm and firm face at my side as he puffed on his pipe and looked contemplatively into the distance.

We went into our tent quite early as we were to make a crack-of-dawn start. Wrapped up in our sheets on two trestle beds we were soon asleep.

While it was still quite dark, I was woken with the smell of hot coffee in my nose. We were up, washed, dressed, and fed in about twenty minutes. A lick and a promise and we were already packing up camp and dousing the still glowing fire while Mohammed warmed up the Rover's engine.

In ten minutes we were aboard, puffing on the first cigarette as Mohammed turned the steering wheel and pointed down the steep rocky valley towards the widening desert. The sun came up away on our left. First a gleam, and then a glowing flashing roseate glare over the dark sky. In the opposite direction the sky changed from indigo to purple then mauve and then a sort of wan blue.

By eight o'clock the heat was beating down and the refreshing though brief dawn was over. We settled down to another scorcher.

This was the first leg of our journey, to see Alan Tyndall, the manager of the Shabluka branch. Alan, a tough little North Country man, was one of those few Englishmen who, like the district commissioners, ruled with a firm though gentle hand, many hundreds of local employees, all of varying tribal loyalties. He was also one of the only men I knew who could speak Arabic fluently and an odd assortment of Riverine and Southern Sudanese tongues with a Yorkshire accent. It was quite disarming.

We remained on a crude path marked and rutted from previous travellers. Along this winding road up a steep grade and there on our right, finally, water. A blue, perfectly gorgeous sparkling canal as far as the eye could see. This was one of the main irrigation canals dug by our company. It was about fifteen or twenty feet wide with well cared for, clean-looking banks, which rose some ten feet above the surrounding countryside.

We drove along on the top of this bank for an hour without going right or left or seeing a single soul. Every so often we would pass a small pump and barge or dam, all untended, but all in good working condition. Away on the other side of the water, the tilled and irrigated ground stretched flat as a billiard table, chocolate brown and neatly furrowed.

In a little while we dropped down off the bank and hit a firm gravelled road that took us through a small village. All the dogs and children came running out, yelling and barking, and trying to keep up with us. We sped through, Mohammed shouting a few niceties at our pursuers.

Down a small hill, round a corner, and there was the Nile ahead. Wide, shiny, and so beautifully wet. Also ahead was the town of Wad Medani, the usual huddle of whitewashed mud huts and native circular tukul huts, a few larger government offices and mercantile edifices, but otherwise unchanged and looking much as it must have to my predecessor during the Mahdist uprising seventy years ago.

This was the slowest part of the trip as we had to honk and crawl our way through the bazaar crowd, donkeys and goats being driven to market, hordes of locals, khaki-clad police, droves of children laughing and waving. Narrow dark overhung streets and alleys, dark nooks, mysterious and cool on all sides, beggars with nameless horrors attached to them roamed blindly in and out of the mob, fighting to keep their feet, beating away cows that roamed equally mindlessly, and threatened to take away their usual pitch in an alley or gutter. The air smelled of burnt wood and cooking fat, incense, and urine, human odour and rotting vegetation. The sun created a miasmic vapour over all, making a visible wall of noxious fragrance.

We finally were through the native quarter and up another small hill, through some gates, and came to a stop. Absolutely bone weary, I stepped out on my side, almost collapsing with fatigue and stiffness. Eric got out, he obviously in much better shape than I, for he leaped up the half dozen steps to accept the hand of Tyndall coming out of the house. It was now about five-thirty in the evening.

"By God, that's what I call timing," said Alan, "just in time for drinks. Ali, whiskey, wa moya (with soda). How do you do. Payne, isn't it? Yes, nice to meet you." His grip collapsed my hand. "You must be tired. Ali has drawn you a cold bath."

Here in Medani things were much as they used to be, no showers or ice or air conditioning. The rooms were even more archaic in their plan than in Khartoum. My room was high and cool, dark with netting over the large bed, a fan circulating over all. Whitewashed walls. Insects buzzing. Cold stone floors. Shutters closed. I threw off my sticky clothes and with relief lay down in the tepid water in the tub.

After lying there a few minutes I got out, and while toweling myself, sipped on the scotch and water someone had mercifully put on the dresser by the bed. I dressed leisurely, lit a cigarette, and went out into the hallway.

This was a large house with a long connecting corridor that gave off into other bedrooms and on to the garden. Through one of these doors, made of glass, framed with white painted wood, I could see as I passed the garden, lush and green flowers, seemingly wild, falling in great profusion down to the river's edge.

As the sun went down, the Nile was gleaming, calm and serene, a felucca breaking its perfection with pointed prow, the water settling in behind, rippling slowly, rustling quietly, with a soft shirring sound like silk being cut with shears.

I went on down the hallway until I found a doorway that led out onto a large veranda where sounds of much loud and boisterous conversation were audible. I found

Eric already out there with Tyndall and wife, a faded but still pretty blonde in her early thirties. She was tired-looking but still very attractive and knowledgeable with strangers, touching her hair and primping, darting here and there, arranging servants' situations as she made the most of visitors seen only once every six months.

We sat and talked and drank while the sun disappeared over the sandy distance, seeming to hiss into the water, and yet it seemed to be at our feet. Soon it was quite dark and we were all quite tight when finally we went in to dinner.

Afterwards Alan wanted to show some films of his last hunting trip, but we were all so tired that it was put over to another time. I sank into bed gratefully, not even bothering to pull the net over my head, and fell into complete oblivion until morning.

We spent the morning inspecting pumping apparatus and the state of our equipment at a large irrigation station nearby, and by noon were ready for a further hundred miles or so into the south. We made our farewells and set out.

Mohammed surprisingly, nursing what I suspected was a bad hangover, caught the tail of the Rover as we drove slowly past the servants' quarters and swung on, cursing under his breath. He sat in the back nursing his head and muttering sullenly under his breath until he fell asleep some twenty miles out in the desert. We made another camp that night and spent a quiet six hours under the stars.

We spent the next few days in much the same way, checking and inspecting, calling on local sheiks and sultans who all had vested interests in irrigating the soil, arguing and cajoling, discussing and disagreeing. Numerous coffees, much greasy chicken, and many sodas were consumed in all these negotiations.

We were then in an equatorial province in the southernmost area of the Sudan, a country of vast rain forests, prolific in game of all kinds, and many tribes. They stood and glared as we drove by, hefting lovingly, short stabbing spears and long wand-like throwing spears. Their little knots of tight hard hair were gathered in bumps over a smooth, otherwise bald scalp, their eyes flashing when you looked away from them and dulling furtively when face-to-face. They too were scarred in the most remarkable patterns.

Eric dropped me off at Juba. He was going on leave and was to spend it with a friend in Kenya. I was to go back with Mohammed by boat. We boarded the El Teb. Mohammed went down to the area set aside for locals and I went up to the promenade deck following a steward to my cabin. He showed me into a tiny but accommodating cabin with a small bunk, washbasin, and closet, two windows shuttered, and that was it. This was to be my home for the next five days, the length of the journey back to Khartoum.

It was just getting to be twilight, such as it was, when a sudden commotion caused me to alter my progress and look over the side. We were casting off. The boat shook as the engines began their thrusting motion and the paddles began to turn, turn, slowly throwing up great bubbling, foaming, churning, brown waters. Slowly we moved away from the jetty amid some cheering and waving. The onlookers were soon indistinguishable.

The shoreline faded away into the dark moist gloom as we chugged away upriver. It was surprisingly cool all of a sudden. A soft whispering breeze had been set up by the boat's motion, and I leaned over the railing well forward and gazed into the darkness ahead. The funnel gave off two mournful hoots from the siren attached, sounding like a braying hysterical donkey. Away in the distance through the river mist, an answering signal came, and at once, watery and faint, I saw two lights, one green, one red, as a sister ship heading south passed on our starboard beam. I remembered the seamanship we were taught and the handling of boats so long ago during the war – "green to green, red to red, perfect safety dead ahead."

I was quite excited by the prospect of the trip and the strange surroundings, but needed more stimulation, or rather more sedation. I went into the bar, ordered a gin, and lit a cigarette. I slept heavily that night, a night full of strange monstrous dreams, queer notions, and weird fancies.

It was light when I awoke, feeling drugged and sleepy. I went down to the dining hall after washing in the tiny space available, and sat down at the table with the rest of the passengers. I hadn't had supper the previous night and I was very hungry in spite of a bad hangover. Mohammed had not yet appeared and I wasn't surprised. He really had been in a bad way last night.

I struggled through breakfast and went out onto the upper deck. Climbing up onto the boat deck just left of the bridge superstructure and near the funnel, I stood and tried to breathe in as much air as I could.

Thick green forests stretched away on either side into oblivion, matted undergrowth marking the great rain forests of the southern Sudan. Now and again a native would be standing out on some mud flat, standing balanced on one foot, the other leg at right angles bent with the foot seemingly attached to the other leg, standing leaning for support on a long spear, with head bent slightly forward, eyes gazing at us as we passed.

We churned and chugged on up river, the great Nile sometimes miles wide, sometimes brushing and cutting through papyrus swamps. The land was home to animals galore: the Sudan wildebeest, the zebra, the gazelle, the rhino and giraffe, all drinking quietly until our presence was noticed, and then they swooped up and away in one graceful velvet motion, running as fast as their legs would carry them back into the bush and grass.

We arrived at Khartoum and Mohammed and I took leave of each other.

I had future occasion to view the whole trip from two different forms of transportation, rail and flight.

We worked and we played tennis, and swam in the limpid green pool at the Sudan Club, and we ogled other men's wives, and got drunk because we had no wives. We stayed out in the sun's heat from noon until four, on the grass with hockey sticks and cricket bats, facing red-faced and perspiring bowlers, with momentary coolness in the pavilion, changing or putting on pads to go out to bat, hearing a somnolent "Good luck old boy" as you went out to the wicket and a "Bad luck old chap" as you came back without glory.

Some sailed on the Nile, some played golf on oiled sand greens where a trap might be full of water and several crocodiles. We went to the cinema sometimes and watched colourful Hollywood. Every Friday and Saturday at the very least we would attend the cabaret, excite ourselves unnecessarily at the gyrations of those untouchable girls, then at one would go to the brothels, if for nothing else than a beer or two and some conversation with Madam One Eye, the most famous Madam between Cairo and Cape Town.

Covering all in those summer days was the heat and sun. It shone all day out of a brazen sky paled in colour because of the strength of the rays beating down and sapping all the strength and will from the spirit and body, mind and soul.

The Sudan Club, which spread its ivory white walls across some several acres, was perhaps the last outpost of the empire of Khartoum. No one other than an Englishman might join automatically, and on the normal payment of certain annual fees, a foreigner might become an honorary member.

The celebrated nights at the club were such as St. George's Day, St. Andrew's Day, Hogmanay, Christmas and Easter. Great feasts were laid and much drunkenness ensued. All the old fights and quarrels between Scots and English, Irish and English, and Welsh and English, were remembered. Gauntlets were cast and fights started, and more often than not, unfinished.

The late autumn was approaching now in this arid

country, and as I had been told, suddenly I woke one morning in late October, feeling a cool breeze blowing through the shutters and jumped up and looked out. After so many mornings of hazy grey blue, presaging days of squalid heat, here was a golden crisp and dewy sunrise. The other unusual thing was that my window faced north and the breeze was coming directly at me. The wind had switched directions, as it always did at this time of year. The wind carried the coolness from Egypt and the sea breezes from the Mediterranean. I threw open the windows and breathed in the type of air and smell that also happens in western countries.

The evenings began to get cool enough that one had to wear suits and long trousers at all times, and as the season progressed, more and more parties were arranged and attended. All the various communities gave balls. The Syrians one night, the Jewish community another, the Italian, the Lebanese, all the commercial enterprises, the tobacco companies, the banking and commercial houses.

These were evenings full of soft drifting music, shadowy shapes on warm moonlit lawns, discreet voices held low, rippling laughter and gestures, half-seen gleaming smiles and errant looks, long dresses, white shirt fronts, and clinking ice-filled glasses, softly moving servants, and trees waving in the late night winds that always came up briefly towards the end of a party, momentarily obscuring the stars and the moon.

I received an unexpected call from Ronald Keymer to meet with him. I arrived at his office. In answer to my tap on the door a gruff voice beckoned me to come in. The pale eyes looked uncomprehendingly at me, inscrutable and staring.

"Ah, yes, yes, Payne isn't it? Do sit down, do sit down. Jolly good. Make yourself comfortable. Well let's see, what do we need you for? I would like you to go and see why some of our bills haven't been paid. Now, here's a list, a little old as you will notice from the dates. We work on the basis that most motor car dealers do so much down and pay the rest from the profit one might make out of the crop of cotton. And these are, to say the least, delinquent. Well, when can you leave?"

"Right away sir."

"Good, clear it with Fairchild. Get a chit for some money and off you go."

As I went out through the door he stopped me.

"Mr. Payne, when you deal with these chaps, please be polite. Forget any ideas you might have been given about the locals. They are gentlemen. Ask about their wives and children and their lives. Have lots of gawa. That's coffee you know."

I did know.

I cleared with Fairchild, went down and found my servant, had him organise the transport, and went off to the mess to pack again. This was to be my first trip into the desert alone or at least without another companion of mine, so I was to try to be as careful as I could, as far as travel requirements were concerned. I took stock. There was me and Ali, my boy. Our transport was a Land Rover, long wheel base type, capable of clearing the deepest sand with its four-wheel drive, and comfortable for four sleepers.

Our trip would last conservatively fifteen days, so I had to draw up rations for that time, plus water, and ammunition for our two rifles, one an ex-British Army Lee-Enfield, the other an Austrian rifle of uncertain vintage, but which had a remarkably long barrel and was very accurate. Ali used this for game.

When I first came to Africa I almost at once went to see the game warden. After setting up an appointment with the department involved, I was called to an appointment. Almost too good to be true, I thought in my youthful cynical way. The building was low long stucco and a form of African thatch. I entered the building by way of some wide stone steps through a veranda shaded by hanging and draping oleander and vivid scarlet wild roses.

"Are you E. A. Payne?" a white-shirted, dark blue tied, grey flannel-slacked Sudani asked, "Would you come this way? Colonel Rogers is expecting you."

He ushered me into a large whitewashed room. All the walls were mounted with the heads of animals of every description. In my relative ignorance I could recognize almost all of them, though perhaps not correctly. There were ibex and Thomson's gazelle and antelope, leopard, lion, and rhino, and many more all set at odd asymmetrical positions on the wall staring out sadly on their tomb. A large ceiling fan revolved slowly, causing some planted palms and Nile bull rushes to stir every few seconds. Behind a dark blackish-brown desk of enormous proportions, on which was spread a rug of Turkish or Persian origin, sat an affable appearing gentleman.

"Won't you sit down Payne? Coffee or Pepsi or Coca Cola?"

"Coffee thank you sir."

The usual handclap followed by the silent entry, the orders given, and the tray whisked in with glass and cup placed before us.

"Well, you want a game license. Well I'm sure we can fix you up. Have you any idea what you want to go after?"

"No, not really. I just feel that while I'm in the country I should have a go."

"Yes. Well you know, I've been a protector of the animals, so to speak, for twenty-one years. What's the most dangerous animal in Africa, would you say?"

I hesitated, I knew it wasn't the lion.

He quickly continued. "I assure you Mr. Payne that *you* are the most dangerous animal here, the only one armed with a high-powered repeating rifle, and the only one who will kill for the sake of fun rather than for food or for danger to one's own beloved ones. You know Payne, that most animals are reasonably docile unless they are wounded or very hungry or in charge of young ones. They are basically suspicious and will run rather than fight."

"We on the other hand will make elaborate preparations to go out and hunt some beast we have never seen and which more often than not has several dependents, so that we can cut off its head, stuff it, mount it, and stick it on the wall. Yes, I notice where you're looking. Well that was my predecessor and I'm having them taken down next week. Now, do you still want the license?"

I refused. He made a definite impression on me.

In the unlikely event that Ali and I ran out of canned food, dried eggs, and Carnation milk, I carried the two rifles, oiled and shiny, together with bandoliers holding sufficient ammo for an army, and had my bags packed and bedding rolls taken into the car. My houseboys helped me load and came down to see me off. I thought they were a bit too sad at my leaving, as if they expected never to see me again.

I drove over to the office building and picked up Ali and we drove off northwards out of town. The road to Shendi, Athara, and the north followed a well-tarmacked straight line. Other than the odd bus and Pepsi Cola stand where warm syrupy drinks were sold in bottles, there was very little sign of life, and very soon, as dusk arrived, even these few landmarks of civilization began to vanish.

The road abruptly ended with a bump and we were out on the open desert again. As far as one could see the horizon stretched in grey-brown monotone like a sepia photograph. At the far right was a conical black volcanic mountain. Smooth at this distance, it stretched up slowly curving to a peak, flat-topped, and down the other side falling to what turned out to be, as we got closer, tumbling black, grey, and brown rocks.

We drove fairly fast. Ali was driving, dipping into softer sand and struggling out the other side in four wheel drive, then jerking and bumping along at fifty on the hard gravel, passing between rocks, skirting dried up river beds that had not seen water since the beginning of time.

At about six that evening, at the base of one of the small rocky hills, we made camp. We were perhaps some sixty miles from the shores of the Nile. The spirit stove was blazing merrily as I washed up after having pitched the tent. Ali was a good cook and a crack shot and a good driver, but his navigational abilities were nonexistent, as was his sense of country living and what might be described as folklore of the desert. It transpired that he was, like me, a city lover and dweller, and had hardly been outside the suburbs of Khartoum in his life.

I laid out our sleeping bags and turned to see how Ali was progressing with the cooking arrangements. All in this department seemed under control. I made myself a scotch and soda and sat down on the collapsible canvas chair I carried everywhere with me. In relaxing, my thoughts turned on the job ahead. We were after these chiefs for the money owed us. I had heard stories of their recalcitrance. What if they turned ugly? What would happen to us if they decided to do away with us? In spite of the warmth of the early evening I shivered.

A great scream made me leap to my feet, drink spilling, eyes wide with shock.

"What the devil?"

Ali had knocked the spirit stove, burning himself nastily in the leg and ruining our dinner in the bargain.

After I'd got over my surprise, the noise from Ali made me think the worst had happened. I dressed his leg as best I could and supported him to his bed. I managed to make some thin soup and this, with some crackers, constituted both our dinners that night. I watched the fire glowing and sputtering as the darkening shadows grew longer and longer, and finally the last spark flickered out leaving us in total darkness. The silence of the night was broken only by an occasional whimpering cry from Ali and the sound of some marauding animal that smelled our fire and food.

I must have dropped off, because the next thing I knew was as if in a dream I felt a rough wetness on my hand or my feet, I cannot be sure which, and a noise of yelling in my ear as if many voices were calling me. I sat up with such a start that the clumsy tan-coloured animal with long twisted horns was startled.

"What in God's name?"

I leaped up and shouted for my gun. The ibex, a great animal of the antelope family and as big as a horse, started away with a grunt of fright and ran across the sand. Ali who was writhing around in pain looked beseechingly at me. I picked up the gun, flicked off the safety, and raised it to my shoulder. Across the greyness of the dawn desert, the animal flickered and disappeared. It was pointless. What use would it be to shoot this beautiful and harmless but curious and hungry beast? I lay the rifle down and shook my head to wake up.

Throwing some water into my face helped. I turned to poor Ali, whose burn was the cause of the shouting. I realised that our trip was to be postponed and that I had to get him to a hospital quickly. He was in bad shape. I dragged him onto the back of the car, settled him in as best I could, and set off to the nearest settlement, which, from the map, lay east and north of us, and was the small river-town of Shendi.

Ali was by now unconscious. It was still dark, though from my watch, morning, and a dawn was very near. I didn't really know what I was going to do or where I was to go for help. There was not, as far as I knew, any British representative here, either official or unofficial. I thought if I drove to the centre of town someone would wake up and help.

Movements were already abroad, thank God, by the time we arrived at the central square. Heavily veiled women in black and blue robes were collecting water and bundles. At our noisy arrival they moved away and covered their faces furtively and nervously, looking over their shoulders as they disappeared into the breaks between huts.

I got out and went around to the back of the Rover. Ali was still out of it. I looked around helplessly at the blank walls surrounding the square. The sun was beginning to peep over some palms across the street, and the street was bathed in a golden glow. Dust began to rise and blow about as a small and practically indistinct morning breeze stirred.

"Ya Said. Ya Said."

I looked around. A very old Arab was beckoning from an aperture in one of the nearer buildings. I approached him. I explained in my bad Arabic that we needed medical help. He stared at me with black eyes, one of which was cast badly as is so common among his people, and which gave him an oddly untrustworthy look.

As suddenly as he had appeared, he vanished. Seconds passed and I turned away wondering again what to do, when our friend reappeared, this time from the doorway and now accompanied by three young stalwart boys. They strode over to the car, looked inside at Ali briefly, then one climbed in and gently helped ease the body out into the arms of the other two standing waiting. He then jumped out and helped them carry Ali into the hut.

I followed with the old man. I was forced to stoop to enter the low and narrow doorway. Although it had become quite light outside it was dark and fetid within. The gleam of a candle came fitfully through the gloom and the heavy weight of sweat and animal odour lay upon the still air, stirred by the movement of the men who carried Ali through the room and helped him towards a bed.

Movements of another kind and sounds of another kind were audible. Grunts and groans. By this time I had become accustomed to the darkness and I could begin to recognize and identify shapes. The room was about ten feet wide and fairly long. There was an aperture at the far end that did service as a window. This was heavily shuttered. There were some beds of the Arabic design in the room. They were made of wood and plaited rope and called "angareebs." On some of them, still sleeping bodies lay. At the far end of the room were some small children grouped, wide-eyed, staring at us with alarm. I pretended not to notice them in the hope that they might become at ease sooner.

We attended to Ali. He was whispering and groaning in the most upsetting manner. The oldest man present, who seemed to be the local soothsayer, administered some potions or ointment to the burns, gave him something to drink, which Ali at once spat and spewed out, then laid a wet cloth dampened with an oddly smelling liquid to the head, and let Ali lay over on his side and sleep.

I found one of the family pressing into my hands a cup of something hot. It smelled greasy and revolting, but it was warm and I was hungry and tired. I took a sip. It was thick but I found it drinkable. I lay down and dozed and then dropped off to a troubled sleep.

I was awoken by a hand gently shaking me. It was the old gentleman. I sat up with a start. It was getting dark again, quite late in the day. I had slept the clock around. All the men of the house were still off working in the fields. Ali and I were alone. Even the children had lost their interest and gone outside to play.

The old gentleman spoke to me in Arabic. He told me that Ali was better and rested enough to carry him back to Khartoum. He ordered his sons, or whoever they were, to carry Ali back out into the car. I rubbed my eyes and straightened my clothes. A bowl of water was given me and I washed some of the sleep away, lit a cigarette and followed the group outside.

The sun was going down fast as it always did. I felt that I would rather stay the night with these people but they obviously didn't want us. After their duties were done it seemed that they wanted to get rid of us as soon as they could.

I thought that at least I could drive maybe thirty miles south and make another camp when it got really dark, and continue the journey the next day to Khartoum, which we should easily make by the following night. While they were making Ali comfortable in the back I checked over the Rover. It seemed in good running order so I warmed up the engine. We still had lots of petrol and water, and our food supplies were hardly touched.

I thanked the villagers for their help – they refused payment. I slipped into gear and rolled slowly down the hard white street. In just a very short time we were out into the open desert. After an hour's drive the night was getting very dark, and finding a couple of shrubs of a thorny nature, but at least affording a little cover, I stopped and dismounted.

I managed to make a nice little camp: a fire burning briskly, Ali set up comfortably with a pillow behind his head, a little food cooking, and bits of the thorn I'd cut up strewn around us to deter any roving beast with soft paws. It was not long after dinner that we were both asleep and snoring soundly.

I woke some time later. I suppose I was over-tired and lay there looking up at the sky, vivid with stars, so close as they always seem to be in these latitudes. My mind whirled and raced thinking about what had happened and how much worse it could have been. The area we were in was not the choicest place to have inconvenient accidents of any sort. I thought about tomorrow and the journey back to Khartoum and how I was to explain why we had to return so soon. Though it had not been my fault I felt vaguely uncomfortable, as though someone else would have organised and arranged things better, or at least differently.

I was just dropping off again when Ali began to snore. In the stillness of the night the sounds he made were magnified and seemed to resound throughout the rocky valley we were camped in. It seemed at certain points that I was about to drift away when my body stiffened and I was wide-awake again. I decided to sit up and have a cigarette and maybe make the fire, which had flickered out by now, and have a cup of tea, when I heard a stone fall, then a small avalanche of pebbles dribbling down the hill. Off to my right another added sound set the hairs on my neck upright, a sound that duplicated Ali's snoring. Snoring and grunting then shuffling steps... then silence.

I jumped up and as quietly as I could, trying to still the sound of panicky breathing, I crept over to where the rifles were in the back of the car. I felt inside in the dark with one eye over my shoulder, found the Enfield, carefully opened the bolt and closed it again with the safety off. I felt my way around to the other side of the car from where the sounds were coming, and waited, trying to be as still and quiet as I could.

Ali was still snoring away happily, when I heard the next sound, feet treading the sand and sprinkling stones, feet that sounded as though they were running. It was now pitch dark and I could wait no longer. I leaped out and with a shout fired a round into the air. There was a sharp crack as another weapon went off, also apparently fired in surprise and panic into the air. A flash lit up momentarily some dark forms and bearded faces. A yell, then stumbling movement, making sounds that quickly diminished into the rocks on either side of our encampment, then silence. I stood half bent in a position of preparedness, waiting for something else to happen, my finger on the trigger. I was by now rather pleased with myself at having driven off what was to become, in later stories, a tribe of the reputedly violent Hadendoa.

It was only after I had stopped shaking and made a cup of coffee for myself, that I found that I had forgotten to reload the rifle and that I had been facing the frightening darkness with an unloaded rifle. I half slept the remainder of the night, one eye cocked for more trouble, until the sun began to cast long and pale shadows amongst the stones and crumbs of the crackling valley we were renting.

As soon as I could see, I made another fire, cooked some water and made more coffee, ate some bread and butter, looked at Ali, who was still groaning and looked rather pale, got into the Rover, cranked her up, and roared off down the ravine towards the desert as though the hounds of hell were after us.

Some four and a half hours later, I began to enter the dusty outskirts of Khartoum. I was not looking forward to reporting my failure to Keymer.

Lost in the desert

Sorting supplies

A party in Khartoum

Another Khartoum house party

Gordon cabaret, New Year's Eve, Khartoum

I had arrived in Africa in July. A year and a half had passed, and the summer and autumn had come and gone twice now. The lovely winter of the desert had also almost run its short life a second time. The winters were cool and sharp, but heartbreakingly short. Timeless days now drifted away into the haze and dust. The occasional March downpour did nothing to alleviate the heat but instead made it sticky. The wind normally in these hot months came from the south, bringing dry arid air, and from time to time from the east, bringing humid water-filled clouds.

Norman Atkinson, Fred Smith and I were at the cabaret a midweek night, when it was quiet. One could get some attention from the girls, a bad hangover for the following workday, and because of the attention, an enormous drink bill at the end of the evening. I was being set upon by a ginger-headed Greek dancer who was asking me for champagne. For kicks Fred had a large Bavarian, flaxen and fat. Norman was closely haggling over the price of the evening.

The days passed fairly contentedly. I was being taught Arabic by a Syrian who called at the mess twice a week and laboriously wrote out the words in a little grey exercise book, to little avail I'm afraid. I could say the very helpful sentence, "Please drive fast as I have to catch the airplane at the airport!" Almost all of anything else escaped me.

We inspected gin mills for cotton, and oil factories, and irrigation schemes, and I fought with London on delivery schedules for the cotton farmer whose crop was dying due to a lack of pumped water because of a spare part needed.

We visited the cabaret and I had my girlfriends. One special favourite was Edna from Hamburg, who would buy one drinks when one was broke, and give cigarettes and small loans to her favourite bachelors. She was a saint and there are few of them amongst the theatricals.

At about this time our plans and thoughts turned to leave time. As this would be my second year in Sudan I had some five months left to be lived through before my leave time came up, but Jack and I were already arranging to spend ours together – three months all told. We had fixed up an extensive grand tour, which was to include Cairo, Rome, the island of Majorca, about which we had heard good reports in that the ratio of men to women was heavily in our favour, and then on to England.

We had seen so many of our friends and colleagues off, enviously, on their leaves over the last several months it was hard to believe that we were at last off ourselves and that we would not be returning to the mess that evening. It was an excessively convivial send off and when we finally were in our seats we were both in a state bordering on paralysis.

We arrived in Cairo at a very early hour that morning and were met by some old friends who worked for BOAC and were now stationed in Egypt. We drove away down a straight, palm-lined boulevard, on one side of which was the continuation of the aerodrome. The row upon row of silver Russian fighter planes sold to the Egyptian government was pointed out to me. An ominous sight with the Middle Eastern tempers running high as they were at that time.

We spent a hilarious ten days and nights night-clubbing, mostly drinking a lot, trying to pick up girls, not too successfully I'm afraid, but enjoying ourselves in the process. However, there still seemed to be something missing. We were really not doing anything particularly different to our usual evening's routine in Khartoum.

Perhaps it would be better in Rome. We embarked once again and arrived at Cianpino Airport in the middle of the day. I was at once disappointed – everything looked so shabby and dingy. I don't know what it was I expected from Italy. My mother being Italian made me want to like it, I suppose.

I had imagined some demi-paradise. Instead, I found it miserably hot, smelly, and noisy. The taxi drivers drove like demented racing drivers – for that matter so did everyone else. I heard later that there were no speed limits on Italian roads. Rome itself was uninspiring, other than the obviously interesting tourist sights. The appetite for life I had read the Italians had, seemed to be rather in their appetite for money and material. The upturned hands and beseeching beggary was exceeded only by what I had already experienced in Egypt. At least there it was done with a certain amount of good humour and dignity.

We had the inevitable experiences one has in places of this sort, meeting the wrong people, drinking the wrong kinds of wine, and eating in the worst as well as the most expensive restaurants. The only girls we met were a couple of students from Cape Town who weren't as interested as we might have believed. Altogether room for improvement we thought. Majorca would be better, it had to be!

We traveled by train from Rome up the coast past Pisa where the tower could barely be seen through a tangle of catalytic cracking plants, oil towers, gasometers, power cables, and other impediments of industry. Up through the Italian Riviera, which was pretty, across the border and into France, along the southern littoral, which was beautiful with its picture postcard colours and views of crashing white breakers, and turquoise sea. Then down to a little harbour where we detrained on the Spanish-French frontier. This was Port Vendres.

It was misty, cold, and very early when we arrived. And almost completely deserted. We struggled with our suitcases across a cobbled yard to a small cafe where we deposited ourselves in an exhausted heap at a zinc-covered bar. In my bad French and Jock's even worse Spanish, we ordered coffee, rolls, and brandy. After this and a cigarette we felt better.

Leaving our cases in the care of the bartender we walked down to the harbour to arrange a passage on the packet that did the short trip to Palma. We found out, to our dismay, that the boat did not leave until ten in the evening, so we got reservations for cabin space and settled down in the bar to kill time.

There was nowhere to go and no other entertainment in the small town, so a good quantity of cognac was consumed that day. Finally it was eight o'clock so we walked as well as we were able to, down to dockside. The ship was a fairly large craft, modern and fast looking, with one sleek raked funnel. We climbed aboard and disposed of our belongings in the small but comfortable cabin. After a wash in the shower, a shave, and change, we took off for the bar.

It was now about nine-thirty and sounds of a ship preparing for sea began above the noise of steam winches and sirens whooping. A military band could also be heard playing in that peculiar shrilling brass-trumpety way of the French army. We looked out of the window of the saloon to see columns of drab-coloured troops tramping down the quay and embarking on a gangplank connected at the afterpart of the ship. We were informed that these were going to Algeria, poor devils.

Although it had been a calm night, upon getting up and having breakfast, the sea began to swell and break as the wind rose. Fortunately for us and our breakfasts, the island was now quite close and we were soon plunging and rolling around the southern headlands and entering calmer sheltered waters just prior to turning north again and entering the breakwater of Palma harbour. We clambered down the gangway encumbered with our luggage, and were set upon by several excessively villainous-looking taxi drivers. After selecting the least objectionable-appearing one, we were escorted with much bowing and saluting to an ancient vehicle of uncertain registry and ancestry. It went much too fast for my sea-strained nerves.

Palma did impress me very much. The beauty of the

Cathedral and market square, the old buildings, as old as most of Rome but so much cleaner, the people themselves possessing apparent character and dignity. We passed by modern hotels and buildings standing cheek by jowl with fourteenth-century buildings and not the least embarrassment. We were deposited with much ceremony at our hotel on the outskirts of the city, overlooking a great sweeping cove with a lovely sandy beach. The weather was lovely, warm, and with a balminess in the air.

The swimming was marvellous, and we had discovered a bar that absolutely oozed with characters, not the least of whom were the proprietors themselves. He was a young Brazilian, looking like a reborn Valentino, she a Nicoise, black-haired, ivory-faced, and ravishing. We spent every night here, after the first meeting.

I had come back to the room one evening, after a day of lounging on the beach and swimming, to find Jock fed up and wanting to go on to Scotland. I was a bit bored too so agreed that we would leave next day. After washing off the salt, I was sipping a drink while Jock was grumbling about the disappointments of the country, with which I was inclined agree. We had been there three weeks and had spent more than we could afford, had not met anyone interesting, nothing important in the way of women, and had not even been screwed.

We were the type that had to have an affair, it was not enough to have a bit, though at this stage of the game that might have pleased us a great deal. So, other than buying the orchestra and dancers champagne in a very bad bar in Palma, we were without experience.

After a bad and greasy meal in the hotel we walked out into the road that ran alongside the low cliff that fell down to the beach and sea. It was a soft warm night, moonlight sparkling off the sea, lights playing around the coast as it curved away on both sides of the bay – much too nice an evening to go to bed early, even for the disillusioned.

Under the cliff right at our feet came music, a samba tickling with dissonance, accompanied by a guitar, the one on record, the other live. Above this came the hum of voices, and clatter of glasses, and laughter and more laughter. We investigated. A narrow path led to steep steps going down and down to what could only be described as a cave carved into the cliff wall. A rude sign on the side of a dimly lit door read Bahia Bar. A curtain of beads covered the doorway.

It was packed with people inside. In a very small corridor-shaped room there must have been over sixty or seventy people. Not too brightly lit, just right, with very small tables, which obliged everyone to stand around and lean against the bar, which ran the full length of one wall.

Behind the bar beamed the owners Oswaldo and Christina. At the far end, painted on the wall was a mural depicting a jungle scene. Netting and lobster traps were draped idly across one another, and dusty plastic flowers completed the attempt at any sort of decor. Not very imaginative or attractive really, but, as in so many cases of this sort, it was the clientele that made the place interesting and exciting, rather like the Duke of Hamilton had been in Hampstead.

After something of a struggle I made it to the bar and asked for drinks. We then retired to the back, and leaning against the lions and rhinos, surveyed the crowd.

It wasn't difficult to pick out the English and Americans. They always stand out in any foreign group, the English being oddly loud and flushed, the Americans, on the other hand, rather quieter and somewhat reticent as though they had read a book on how to behave in other countries. Their accents gave them away.

The French, quite dour, like dark Scotsmen sipping their Cuba libres furtively, the Scandinavians quite jolly and extroverted, especially the Swedes who are supposed to be the other way around, and the Danes in spite of what one hears of Copenhagen and the Tivoli Gardens, fairly plain, homely, and wanting to please. The Norwegians were quite wild. The Germans and Northern Swiss were smiling in rather a contemptuous manner at everyone. It was quite an education.

I felt immediately at home here and when Oswaldo fought his way through the crowd to fetch me and Jock and take us to meet some new friends who he described, shouting to be heard above the din all about, how I would like them because one of them was so beautiful and to Jock that he thought one of the Danes was a bit dodgy. All this in a mixture of Portuguese, English, and Spanish, which he always fell into when slightly drunk and excited.

He was a lovely man, good looking and with a personality to suit. He was also extravagantly generous. He and Christine were madly in love and were constantly looking at each other and practically licking their lips. He led us to the other end of the bar where the English couples I had noticed on entering, were, but now there was someone else with them. There stood the beautiful woman Oswaldo had mentioned. He had not done her justice. She turned away from someone who was making her laugh and looked directly at me. She was unbelievably lovely and I was captivated. She smiled.

As we were introduced I didn't hear any of the names or any of the polite chatter that accompanies these conventions. I could only stare at her like a schoolboy.

She motioned to me to sit next to her. I did, and the rest of the world disappeared. She also emanated a glow of warmth and I felt enveloped in this combination of personal charm and physical attractiveness. She smelled of the beach, salty, clean, and an odd heady combination of wine from her breath and a lovely perfume. She was tanned and had brilliant clear eyes, soft and gentle, her hair long, luxuriant, and auburn. I couldn't help but notice her smashing figure too.

The night went on 'til dawn broke. She was leaving the next day to visit another village further up the coast. She was a model. She was from New York City and had just finished a show in Cannes. She was now on holiday with her son. Ah, here's the rub, here's the catch, but wait, she's caught in a loveless marriage. That's better. Oh, I must be careful and compassionate and strong. I pitied myself terribly. A shoulder was needed, no sudden moves of an over anxious nature – certainly nothing sexual.

We left each other at the door of the bar. She went down the little street with her English friends, and my heart went with her. I fell into bed and slept like a child until noon, full of myself. I woke Jock up. He had left the bar early last night with a French sailor. Because of the way society was in those days, it came as a complete surprise to discover that Jock was gay. He had never ever indicated any sort of inclination one way or the other. I always thought him sexless. Before I could say a word about my adventures of the night, he had broken down and was sobbing.

It all came out, the whole sad tale. I thought that the frustrations must have been dreadful for him, as for others in the same situation in those unforgiving days. The incident last night with the matelot had been his first affair for some time. It ended sadly. I tried to comfort him.

All of us bachelors lived like priests in the Sudan. We certainly lived without any sexual comfort. For normally randy men in our twenties this was a hard regime to follow, but in any case, the slip, as he thought it, was weighing heavily on his conscience.

Jock was a Scottish Catholic who looked like Tarzan. He was a complex mixture, liable to explode. When he composed himself we went down to the bar and spent the rest of the afternoon and evening catching up with each other. We became and remained close friends for the rest of our time together. After several years had passed and we had parted I heard that he had died in a swimming accident in Tokyo Bay. As I knew that he was a masterful swimmer and was very strong I suspect that life had probably become unbearable for him.

The next day I was determined to find my queen of the night before. Her name was Laura. Jock came with me, his normal boisterous self. We drove in the little rented Renault along winding precipitous coastal roads, the sea crashing against rocks below. I wasn't uncomfortable with heights then. Then over a rise, and the road descended sharply to the sea, which glittered in the sun. We drove down, and into the small village of Formentor.

I looked for, and found, the hotel she had mentioned. The lobby was cool and pleasant inside after the noonday heat outside. I questioned the clerk about Laura. He told me she was on the beach. We followed him out and across the road. He pointed vaguely in the direction of the sand, from which sounds of children laughing and squealing came. Walking down to almost the waters edge we looked up and down.

I turned, and then I saw her. She was laying, sun bathing, and had been hidden by a large orange sunshade. She saw me as I approached and the look of pleasure on her face quickly changed to alarm as she looked at me. I turned to see a young boy coming toward us.

"Hi Mom. The water is fun!" He looked enquiringly at Jock and me.

"Bruce, these are some new friends," said Laura calmly. We shook hands. He flopped down on the sand and began drying himself. He chattered away, with his mother occasionally glancing up at me, but quickly looking away when she caught my eye. I wished the ground would swallow me up. This was not a comfortable moment.

Bruce disappeared to get a soda and I immediately started to apologise. Laura explained that although it was a surprise, she was glad I came. I nodded towards the direction the boy had taken...

"Don't worry. Bruce is very grown up for his age. I was just startled when I first saw you."

That night we all had dinner and I found myself getting on well with Bruce. Jock was looking very happy now and obviously was enchanted by Laura. We eventually said our goodbyes and Jock and I left to drive back to our hotel.

It was the day after that Jock was leaving for Scotland. I went to the airport to see him off, watched the plane take off and disappear. I returned to the hotel to pack my bag.

I was moving in with Laura and Bruce. That night then began one of the happiest weeks of my life.

We all had separate rooms but every night Laura and I made love. We lay on the beach and swam, she bought me snorkel gear complete with spear gun, which I quickly made useless by losing the spear in the bay chasing a grouper. We had wonderful lunches on the veranda of the hotel attended closely by a horde of waiters. Laura attracted the attention of men like a magnet. We took siestas until the sun set, when we again sat on the terrace drinking the sharp Majorcan wine. Then dinner, then to bed with the breeze of the night causing the palm fronds outside the windows to brush against the shutters.

The sad day had to come. She was leaving for a few days in Paris. I had to go to London to report to head office and to continue my leave. We arranged to meet for a few days in Paris. She was then returning to America by passenger cargo ship. We said our goodbyes, hugged and kissed. Bruce and I had become close by now and I was sorry to have to leave them both.

I left Majorca by sea to return to Rome the way we had come. The trip was uneventful. During the next leg of my journey I was traveling first class on the train, which was very agreeable, and met some interesting people from South Africa. The time passed pleasantly.

In London I was staying with George, who opened the door of his Hampstead flat with a broad grin. God, it was good to be home. It was just as if I'd never left. The same old faces just three years older. The same predictable comments from Gwenda, who still nursed a grudge I think.

After spending a jolly couple of hours at the pub we staggered back to George's flat where he made me a thick bacon sandwich. Nothing had changed. We slept.

I had about two weeks leave left and part of that was spent visiting some factories in Lincolnshire, people we represent in the Sudan. I was made much of. It was fun being treated with such deference and respect as was accorded me. The next few days flew by.

Then there was Paris...

I don't remember any salient points, as the two days passed in a blur of happiness at being together, but with the shadow of impending parting always on the horizon. We had rented a room in the attic of an old house on the Left Bank. It looked out over the shiny wet roofs of the city and was all too romantic and sad for words.

I saw her off at the Gare du Nord where she was taking the train for some port in Belgium to get the boat for the United States. With that peculiar squeak that the locomotives of the French state railways make, heralding departure, the train creaked and groaned into action. Laura waved out of the window until the train disappeared around the bend.

I walked back to the streets in tears...

Jock

At La Cabana with Jock, Laura, and friends

wings burning fast returning
sad eyes smile and windows opening

snow wilting snowdrops climbing
water melting ice behind

frozen crisp behind the sky
greeting clouds that rain and dry

sunbeams
panes crack
grass green and laughter back...

I felt myself shaken awake. I was in the middle of a delectable dream. Laura and I were on the beach and she was saying something...

"Teddy Teddy."

No it was more like, "Effendi Effendi."

I opened my eyes to see this black face, white teeth bared in an enormous happy smile.

It was dear Ali with a cup of tea, which steamed away on the bedside table.

"You will be late. It is a half past eight."

"Christ. Thanks Ali." I leapt out of bed and got under the shower. Ali followed me with the teacup which he held for me while I sipped and soaped at the same time.

The day was already hot and the water evaporated in no time. I was quickly dry. Dressing in the usual way, I ran down the stairs pausing only to grab a hard-boiled egg and a slice of toast. I was out the door and into the Vedette.

I had arrived late the night before and had been kept up 'til late by all the lads who wanted news of old England, starved as they were. Four field engineers had returned on the same flight with me, and one of them, Dick Francis, made us howl at some if his tales. Apparently when he arrived at his house somewhere in some northern city he knocked on the front door standing in the pouring rain and waited some not inconsiderable time until the door finally opened. It was his mum, dish in one hand with dishcloth in the other, "Oh 'allo Dick," she said. I should mention here that he had not been home for ten years.

It had now been almost a month since the last letter from Laura and I was becoming increasingly despondent. I was drinking too much, not sleeping, and generally behaving in a bloody-minded manner to my friends and fellow workers. I had several times got into complicated situations over planned projects, and I saw Ali giving me reproachful looks, which coming from this gentle soul was the epitome of a severe scolding.

I was determined to do something drastic. I would phone her. The telephone call would go overland to Cairo, by cable under the sea to Calabria, then overland to Rome, to Paris, overland and under the channel to London, and to New York by trans-Atlantic cable.

I went to Eric's room to use his phone. We had both been drinking scotch, me for courage, him to help put up with my bleating. I went through the process of dialing, and in a remarkably short time, heard the ringing at the other end of the earth. The receiver was picked up and I heard her voice.

"Hello."

The overseas operator said, "I have a call from a Mr. Edward Payne."

There was the briefest pause.

Laura simply said, "I don't know any Edward Payne."

Work and every-day life went by in a daze. Everything seemed unimportant and meaningless. I was at a complete loss as to what to do. A letter arrived two or three days later from her to say in the most casual and cold way that I should forget her, that she was staying with her husband. What had seemed like a wonderful dream in the romantic ambiance of the Mediterranean was, under the cruel grey light of New York, an awful nightmare.

I was determined that I would resign and go to the Unite States. My sister was there; she had married and was now living in the Midwest. She had always encouraged me to join her. I would go there and try to convince Laura that she would have a better life with me.

Where I got the gall to come up with this preposterous idea I can't think, as I had no money, no real professional trade or acumen. My prospects were dim indeed, but the drive to see her again was too strong for any sense to be made. Needless to say everyone was totally taken aback. I was giving up a promising career. I was mad to throw it all away and go off into the unknown. Of course I didn't tell Keymer the truth. He would not have understood. He was in fact sympathetic to my desire to join my sister in America.

All my mates on the other hand were incredulous. I had to give six months' notice so it was for the early winter of the following year that I had made all my arrangements.

I found myself eventually in the bar at the

Khartoum airport having a quick one with the chums I'd made over the years. The announcement had just been made that the flight was about to board, when the bar door opened and Ezzel Din came in and approached me.

"All your Sudani friends are outside, they want to say "ma salaam." (...which means goodbye.)

I followed this wonderful man into the hall to find it packed with all the boys I had worked with, Ali from stores, Ahmed, Mohamed, all the people I had been so close to who had helped me and had protected me, laughed with me, and travelled the length and breadth of this strange fascinating country.

Struggling to control the emotions that were causing me to choke, and then realizing that they intended to put me on their shoulders, I protested, but they were determined. I was hoisted up like a baby and carried in a great roaring riotous mob to the plane. I couldn't help noticing with satisfaction, the looks of disapproval from other Brits on their way to the plane.

Enormous hugs, kisses, tears, eyes bright and sad. Hands touching me, pulling me as if to prevent me going, all very sad and disturbing, I knew I would never see them again and they did too. I see them now, their beautiful black faces scarred with their tribal and ritualistic incisions, mouths open wide in brilliant white shouts of farewell.

I settled in my seat in a state of complete collapse. Much later, after several drinks and dinner that I could hardly finish, I fell asleep and slept fitfully until the plane was preparing to land at Rome airport. I had to pull myself together. After the send off, the finality of all I was doing was sinking in.

I began to stew about the future. I have always found it difficult to think things through, to analyze and contemplate situations in a sensible way. My decisions in life have either been guided by my instincts or by someone else who is in some way deeply involved, like joining up, coming to Africa, and now going to America, quite enormous, and, for someone who is as timid as me, quite brave. I sat up, lit a cigarette and ordered a scotch and water.

I spent a couple of days in London, saw my chums, and spent almost all my cash on a riotous night at the Duke.

Next day, feeling like death warmed up, I boarded the BOAC DC6 to New York. There had been a weather delay in London at take off, which I hadn't noticed. An uneventful flight of some considerable length followed – at least it was uneventful until we reached the North American coast. The pilot had just told us we were coming up on Labrador. It was getting close to dusk, when, out of nowhere, there appeared on my side of the airplane, a jet fighter aircraft. It was so close one could see the pilot.

There was a ripple of excited conversation throughout the cabin as everyone speculated on the meaning of this mysterious apparition. Our pilot said in matter-of-fact tones that it was the Yanks having a look at us. It was the height of the Cold War, so this sort of occurrence was apparently routine. The jet wagged its wings and then soared away into the rapidly darkening eastern sky.

We were now flying over land and what I could see was magnificent and strange. The land mass stretching away into the distance was chocolate-coloured with ripples of white, where the snow lay in creases and valleys and where drifts had collected. In the middle background, foothills progressed into mountains. A cold and motionless world lay below. The whole impression was one of great power and indifference. The sky then went black and the landscape disappeared into the night.

When we landed, I made my way to the BOAC office. The banks were closed, so I was hoping that they would cash me a cheque. This was before the days of credit cards. The only, other way of transacting money matters was by traveller's cheques, which I didn't have. The BOAC people were splendid.

The arrival at New York was late, thus they felt it was their responsibility so they put me in charge of a BOAC officer who took me by cab to Manhattan, which he paid for. He checked me into a room at the Prince George Hotel and practically tucked me in bed all on the house.

My first thought on waking was that I should call Laura. It was going to be delicate. As far as she was concerned I was still several thousand miles away and I didn't want to give her a heart attack. Also, what if he answered? Well I had to take a chance. I dialed the number.

After a couple of rings she answered. I must admit that the bad side of me got some satisfaction from her reaction. After the initial shock she was, to my surprise, quite warm, and spoke with affection. She started to make excuses, but I interrupted her to suggest that we meet and have a face to face, especially as this might be the last time, and I had come a long way. She agreed, albeit with reluctance. She said to meet her in the lobby of the Plaza Hotel at noon.

After a quick breakfast I got to the bank by cab, gazing around with amazement and wonder.

It so often happens when one goes somewhere new and foreign, that disappointment is experienced. This was not true of New York. If anything, it was even more extraordinary than description and picture had prepared me for. It was a brilliant winter day and the buildings stood out in pristine clarity against the hard blue sky.

I got the banking done and walked and walked, absorbing the sights sounds and smells that were capturing my senses with their unusual variety and magic. I waved a taxi down and told him where I wanted to go.

He twisted around and said "Jeez, that's around the corner."

When I explained that I didn't know the city, he smiled and said, "You're a limey ain't cha?" I agreed that I was, and he said, "Jeez, I was over there in forty-two in the U.S. Army. Hey how about me showing you round the city?"

I mentioned my perilous financial position.

He said, "Hey, no charge. You guys were real good to me over there. Jeez I almost married a limey."

Well this was alright. I still had an hour to go before

the date with Laura so I agreed.

Leaning forward so that I could hear everything he said, we spent the next hour sightseeing. When he dropped me off at the Plaza I offered him five dollars from my precious and precarious coffers, but he sheepishly refused and gruffly bid me luck. I thought, if this is typical of American behaviour, I was going to like it here.

I climbed the steps of the hotel, which I had heard of, and a magnificent doorman saluted and smiled a welcome. Through the revolving doors and into splendour. It quite took my breath away. After the sparseness of the Sudan, both in its geography and its architecture, this was almost too rich to bear.

The encrustations of gold, swages of lush velvet draperies, embellishments of gilt paneling of rare and exotics woods, porters and waiters, bell boys with little pill box hats on their heads, scurried here and there. The objects of all this attention stood and sat about, dressed to the hilt with obviously expensive and stylish garments, expensive perfumes mingled with aromatic tobacco smoke, furs everywhere. Total and spectacular excessiveness held sway.

I had waited just a few minutes when Laura walked up to me. God she was still exquisite. Tall, slim, her hair long and lustrous, eyes wide and bright with pleasure. We kissed... . It was as though we were back in Majorca, no time had passed, and I was convinced she still loved me.

I was rooted to the floor, stammering and clumsy. Get a grip Ted!

We walked hand in hand. She suggested we get a

drink and pointed to the nearby bar entrance. As we approached, the host remarked that ladies were not allowed in the Oak Room 'til five in the evening.

Laura replied with some alacrity that she was no lady.

"In that case, come in madam," he said with a grin.

Damn, I loved this woman.

We sat and drank and talked and laughed and held hands. I was captivated and spellbound. It all seemed to be going so well.

We had been together for an hour or so when she announced a need to powder her nose. While she was gone, I ordered another round. We were drinking martinis, which I was not used to, so was feeling quite light-headed. She seemed gone a long time and I was beginning to get worried, when she suddenly appeared. Her face had changed and she had become very business like.

"I've got to go."

This was a different Laura. This was Laura Domesticus. "I've all sorts of stuff to do: shopping for dinner. Bruce and Dick will be expecting to be fed."

This was the first time she had mentioned her son and husband. It cooled my ardour quickly. I got up and brushed peanut dust from my suit.

"Don't bother to see me out."

A waiter hovered. Suddenly the atmosphere changed from light-hearted affection with definite promise, to one of briskness and distance.

"No, wait, let me pay the bill and I'll come with you."

She hardly waited for me as I settled the bill and I had to almost run to catch up with her. This was not at all how I had pictured this episode. It was all so undignified and unpleasant. She paused at the revolving door, lifted her face for me to peck at her cheek and said, "Sorry this couldn't have worked," and was gone.

I followed through the door and watched her descend the steps and enter the crowds on the pavement. I thought, if she turns around there might still be a chance... She didn't. Laura disappeared into the throng. I returned to my hotel in deep depression.

Laura at Idlewild Airport
(now JFK Airport, NYC)

I got through the night somehow, and next day managed to get a flight to Chicago where I was to catch a Greyhound bus to the town in Wisconsin where Madeleine now lived with her family. The flight took off in a snowstorm, which alarmed me considerably, but upon reaching a certain altitude, broke through heavy clouds into a star-lit beautiful clear night. I had dinner and went to sleep nursing my bruised and broken spirits.

Chicago came, and I transferred by cab to the bus station. It was now quite late and snowing heavily. I had never seen snow like this in my life, and found it, at the same time awesomely lovely and a cause for some consternation, especially as the driver drove, I thought, rather too fast. But he was no doubt an expert at his job, so I made a pillow of my jacket and went to sleep.

I slept fitfully until waking to feel the bus sliding sideways on the icy road. By then wide awake, I looked around to see that we were in what looked like a suburban street and were lodged up against a tree. So much for the expert driver.

There was some commotion in the bus and we all finished up on the snowy icy street where, under the orders of someone who seemed to know what he was doing, we managed to get ourselves covered with snow, dirt, and diesel fumes in an unsuccessful attempt to move the bus.

In what seemed like hours later, a service truck

arrived and got us going. We continued our journey now
with eyes wide open.

After a few more interminable hours of tobaccoed
air, the atmosphere in the bus was by now quite foul, being
made up, in roughly equal parts, along with body odour and
cheap spirits. My mouth felt dry and I was dying for a
shower. We seemed to be arriving at our destination.

"Fort Atkinson!" the driver called out.

The bus swung into a yard and came to a heavy
stop. As I edged my way forward, I could see Madeleine
and Bob, her husband, waving and smiling. It had been too
long. It was lovely to see them again and we were all talking
a mile a minute with all the catching up to do.

Bob drove deftly and in no time we drew up to a
sweet little cottage. Two children were looking out of the
window. The lights inside shone onto the snow outside, a
cat ran out and jumped into Madeleine's arms. The whole
scene was like something out of a Norman Rockwell
painting. I was to spend three very happy years there...

The screw in the DC3's engine still revolved, but I
ignored it now, having accepted what the flight attendant
told me. Something else seemed to be happening. The
undercarriage was being lowered. I looked at my watch. We
would be arriving at Grand Rapids soon, where I would
start my new work. As the thought crossed my mind, we

began to descend through the clouds.

That first flight to Khartoum seemed so long ago now, the nervousness, the boiled sweets, the missionary lady. Now I was a seasoned flyer.

The undercarriage grumbled down and clumped into locked position. We banked gently and went into a final glide. The clouds thinned out, and suddenly all the little buildings appeared, toy cars, rail lines and power masts all flashing by. A bump, a squeal, a bounce. Now adhesion and braking.

With a slight tremor, the tail wheel dropped to the ground and the DC3 adopted its nose-up tail-down position and taxied toward the airport buildings.

We were cleared through quickly and I walked toward the car park. I was feeling a bit down, and then I realised with a little frisson of pleasure, I had a date that night. My clouds lifted and I was reminded for some reason of the only joke that stayed with me in all the years I had spent in the Middle East and Africa...

"When will you pay me the money you owe me?" asks one Arab of another.

"Tomorrow."

"Tomorrow?... yes, when the apricot blooms in the desert."

Edward Payne's roots are in Constable country, the counties of Suffolk and Norfolk in eastern England. He completed his formal art education in Norwich and London. Edward currently lives in Stratford, Ontario where he continues to pursue his success as a gifted watercolour artist along with his writing. He has completed volume two of his memoirs, *The Streets of Odeon,* has done a book of narrative and watercolour titled *Teddy Payne's Stratford,* and is nearing completion of a novel set around the time of the First World War, as well as other literary projects.

Also by Edward Payne...

available from

fanfare books

92 Ontario Street,
Stratford, ON, N5A 3H2

519.273.1010
fanfare@cyg.net